How to Save Your Neighborhood, City, or Town

How to Save Your Neighborhood, City, or Town

The SIERRA CLUB Guide to Community Organizing

by Maritza Pick

SIERRA CLUB BOOKS · SAN FRANCISCO

8-15-03

The Sierra Club, founded in 1892 by John Muir, has devoted itself to the study and protection of the earth's scenic and ecological resources—mountains, wetlands, woodlands, wild shores and rivers, deserts and plains. The publishing program of the Sierra Club offers books to the public as a nonprofit educational service in the hope that they may enlarge the public's understanding of the Club's basic concerns. The point of view expressed in each book, however, does not necessarily represent that of the Club. The Sierra Club has some sixty chapters coast to coast, in Canada, Hawaii, and Alaska. For information about how you may participate in its programs to preserve wilderness and the quality of life, please address inquiries to Sierra Club, 730 Polk Street, San Francisco, CA 94109.

LIBRARY OF CONGRESS CATALOGING-IN-PUBLICATION DATA
Pick, Maritza, 1951–
    How to save your neighborhood, city, or town: the Sierra Club Guide to community organizing / by Maritza Pick
        p.   cm.
    Includes bibliography.
    ISBN 0-87156-522-6
    1. Green movement—Handbooks, manuals, etc. 2. Advertising campaigns—Handbooks, manuals, etc. 3. Advertising, Political—Handbooks, manuals, etc.
    I. Sierra Club. II. Title.
    HC79.E5P514 1993
    363.7'057'0973—dc20   92-25143
                                                               CIP

Production by Robin Rockey and Susan Ristow
Cover design by Paula Schlosser
Book design by Paula Schlosser
Illustrations by Alexander Laurant

Printed in the United States on acid-free paper containing a minimum of 50% recovered waste paper of which at least 10% of the fiber content is post-consumer waste.

10   9   8   7   6   5   4   3   2   1

*HC
79
.E5
P514
1993*

"Never doubt that a few committed individuals can change the world. Indeed, it is the only thing that ever has."

—MARGARET MEAD

CONTENTS

ACKNOWLEDGMENTS

This book is dedicated to my parents, Mila and Moritz Pick, who taught me to cherish democracy—the freedom to make this a better world than we found it. Thanks are due to my brother, Lenard Pick, with whom I learned to worship nature as we romped in open meadows and orchards near our childhood home. Once a rural town of 4000 people, the setting of my fond memories has long since become an overcrowded city with more than 100,000 people. The land is crammed to bursting with tract houses, the streets choked with traffic, the air poisoned by toxic dump fumes, and the surrounding mountains cloaked in a bleak curtain of smog. My childhood paradise has disappeared; it lies buried in an asphalt grave. I lost one paradise. I became an activist because I do not intend to lose another.

There comes a time when we all must take a stand to struggle for the survival of what we love. That time is now.

I thank all the friends who joined me in our many victorious environmental battles.

My editor, Jim Cohee, and Sierra Club Executive Director Michael Fischer demonstrated instant enthusiasm for this book. Their encouragement was a writer's dream come true.

I feel special gratitude to wise political sage Ken King, who showed me the many paths to environmental victory. By his example, I learned to smile graciously while stirring up trouble at city hall.

This book could never have been written without the steadfast encouragement of my husband, André. He used to say, "Visualize how powerful the environmental movement would be if environmental groups gave this book to each of their members. Imagine millions of well-prepared men and women fighting to save our Planet Earth! What a grand spectacle!" That spirit made this book possible.

PART I

How to Organize Your Community to Solve Environmental Problems

CHAPTER 1

How to Begin:
An Activist Is Born

A bomb has just dropped on your neighborhood. It will change your life forever. Yet you first learn about this bomb from a short article in the local paper. The small headline hidden on the back page reads: "Plan to Build 1000 Apartments on Pastoral Lane." The article briefly describes the gigantic shopping center, community hospital, roller-skating rink, and new fire station that will accompany the one thousand apartments proposed for the undeveloped pasture where cows now graze. You have lived on quiet, rural Pastoral Lane for twenty years. You panic. This development would destroy your way of life forever.

Perhaps you just moved to a lovely new city and discover that a nuclear power plant, closed for years, is suddenly slated to reopen. In your nightmares, your spouse develops an eerie radioactive glow.

Any number of back-page newspaper items could cause your Sunday breakfast to curdle in your stomach. You read in the newspaper about Mr. Pillar-of-Society, the main proponent of the particular project. Mr. Pillar-of-Society is a shining asset to your community. He is a leader in the local chamber of commerce and coaches Little League baseball in his free time. Yet, this Mr. Pillar-of-Society wants to destroy your life. Who is this individual, really? Your panic escalates.

You read the newspaper article a few more times as your blood pressure rises. Furious, you rip out the article and head for the front door. Forgetting that you are still wearing your Sunday slippers and morning robe, you charge down your peaceful little street and knock on the first door.

"Have you read this?" you gasp at your neighbor.

Congratulations! You have just taken your first step to becoming a community organizer. Every person's natural reaction is: "How can they get away with this?" However, a potential community organizer's natural response goes one step further: "I won't let them get away with this! But how to stop them?"

The bomb can explode in an infinite variety of bad news. Instead of a shopping center and high-density housing complex, you might read that a new airport is planned for the meadow near your home. Perhaps a lumber company purchased the nearby forest and intends to spray dangerous herbicides. Maybe your tap water tastes odd. You and your neighbors worry that your town's groundwater has been contaminated by leaching from the local garbage dump. Perhaps the factory across town is spewing out poisonous fumes. You observe your withering vegetable garden and suspect a connection. Perhaps you love fishing and the trout population has declined suddenly in your favorite lake. Maybe you remember the days when the community beach never needed to be posted with the sign: "Stay out of the water! May be hazardous to your health!" Who is responsible? What do you do?

Your home may be an apartment, a condominium, a farm, a ranch, a beach cottage, a woodsy cabin, a mobile home, or a suburban house. Wherever you live, when an environmental crisis strikes your community, you must take a stand to defend your values. The purpose of this book is to show you how to organize to win these battles. This book is a step-by-step practical guide to environmental victory.

Throughout this guidebook, you will encounter the hypothetical developer, Mr. Pillar-of-Society. Insert your particular community's problem in place of Mr. Pillar-of-Society's development. Crises vary, but effective means of organizing to deal with these crises remain amazingly constant.

Whatever your environmental problem, you will need to know: how to create and run a community organization; how to deal with your mayor, city council, county supervisors, and other public officials; how to obtain press coverage for your cause; how to network with other local and national organizations; how to prepare for public hearings; and how to run a successful election campaign to place your allies in local political office—in short, how to win.

How to Notify Your Community

Many of your neighbors have missed the article in the newspaper that has sent you through the ceiling with worry. Other neighbors may have read the article, yet they don't believe that there is anything that they can do against Mr. Pillar-of-Society's development proposal. Mr. Pillar-of-Society is rich and influential. He has friends on the city council. He contributes generously to the county supervisors' campaigns. Most of your neighbors are ready to be defeated without a fight because they don't think a fight is even possible. They take the news of the proposal as if it were a fact that they simply have to live with, no matter how much they hate it.

Most community organizations begin with just one person. Let's say that you are this one person. The first thing you have to do is to notify your community of the development and your opposition to it.

Prepare a one-page "Dear Neighbor" letter. The letter must be neatly typed without typographical errors. On the top in bold letters you might want to underline "Neighborhood Alert." Use a copy machine at your local print shop to copy your letter onto brightly colored, eye-catching paper. A poorly copied, messy, or handwritten letter will probably be tossed into the trash without being read by your neighbors.

On one sheet of paper, type up succinctly the most alarming aspects of the development and its consequences to your community: noise, air pollution, traffic, destruction of wildlife, high-density housing, a complete change from a quiet neighborhood to an urban center. Be graphic. In a couple of paragraphs, make it clear to your neighbors that their entire way of life is threatened. Put your telephone number on the letter. You may want to leave your name off the letter, or you may just give your first name. At this stage you are probably nervous about how much of a public figure you want to be. You may never have been involved in political organizing before. You may be a quiet person who values your privacy. Don't worry. You can become a political organizer and still maintain your privacy. Tell people to call if they are concerned about the development proposal. List the hours when they can best reach you. If you don't already have a telephone answering machine, then it's time to buy one.

When people call you, write down everyone's telephone

number and address in order to contact them for future meetings. Put a star by the names of callers who strike you as particularly articulate or knowledgeable. Put a different kind of marking by the names of those who sound like crackpots. Every community has its share of hotheads. But they too can play a useful role in your future organization. Don't discount them right off the bat.

Following is a sample "Dear Neighbor" letter that an individual might write regarding her concern about a nearby factory that is spewing harmful chemicals into the air through its smokestack and dumping hazardous waste into the groundwater supply.

★ ★ ★ *NEIGHBORHOOD ALERT* ★ ★ ★

Dear Neighbor:

Have you noticed that plants in your garden don't grow as well as they used to? Does your tap water taste peculiar? For some time I have been very concerned about the acrid taste of our tap water. I have also watched my flower and vegetable garden die on the vine. I wonder why. Don't you?

I would like to discover the cause of these problems. I worry that air and water pollution in our community might lead to serious health problems for ourselves and our children.

If you are also concerned, please contact me at 888-8888. I am best reached between six and nine in the evenings. If you reach my answering machine, please leave your name and telephone number so that I may call you back.

Together, as a neighborhood, we may be able to uncover the source of our air and water pollution and put a stop to it. It is important for our health and our children's health that we get to the bottom of what is poisoning our air and groundwater.

Cordially,

Your neighbor, Susan D. Scared

Perhaps you have progressed beyond fear and are downright furious. The following is a sample "Dear Neighbor" letter from a person who is sick and tired of garbage washing up on his favorite nearby beach.

★ ★ ★ *NEIGHBORHOOD ALERT* ★ ★ ★

Dear Neighbor:

Are you angry about the trash that washes up on our beaches? Are you sick of finding hypodermic needles, empty syringes, mysterious plastic bags, and all kinds of other garbage cluttering up our shores? Are you tired of seeing signs posted: "Warning: Swimming in this water may be hazardous to your health"? Then let's put our anger to good use and do something to clean up our beaches.

I would like to start a neighborhood organization to deal with the problem of trash on our beaches. Please join me so that we may once again enjoy swimming and fishing off our beautiful shore.

I think we must contact our city council members and our waste-disposal companies to find out who is responsible for the destruction of our beaches. We must demand a halt to the devastation of our wonderful natural treasures.

Please give me a call if you want to stop the transformation of our beaches into garbage dumps. Nobody else in our town is doing anything about it. It is up to you and me.

Sincerely,

Your neighbor, Fred B. Furious
Telephone number: 222-2222

You may want to present your "Dear Neighbor" letter as a fact sheet. The following is a sample leaflet that might be created by neighbors worried about a nuclear power plant that may be reopened in their hometown.

★ ★ ★ *NEIGHBORHOOD ALERT* ★ ★ ★

FACT: Three years ago, the nuclear power plant in our town was closed down because of repeated malfunctions that made it too dangerous to keep open.

FACT: It cost you, me, and all of us taxpayers millions of dollars to build a faulty nuclear power facility that endangered all of us.

FACT: Our gas and electric bills are now much higher than the national average because we're paying for the mistake of building the malfunctioning nuclear power plant in the first place.

FACT: Political forces are pushing to reopen the nuclear power plant.

We can't let the lobbyists for the nuclear power industry get away with another boondoggle at the expense of our tax dollars and our community's health.

Meet at my house at 111 Nonuke Lane on Wednesday evening, February 12, at 8:00 P.M. for a neighborhood meeting to discuss how to organize to oppose the reopening of the nuclear power facility.

For more information, call me, Shirley Doright, at 111-1111. ONLY OUR INVOLVEMENT CAN SAVE OUR TOWN!

How to Distribute Your Letter

Let's say you are still a one-person organization. With luck, you may have a friend, spouse, or child who is willing to help you distribute the "Dear Neighbor" letter. How you distribute your letter depends largely on the type of neighborhood in which you live. In all likelihood, you won't want to spend a lot of money for postage at this point. Plus you don't need the added cost of buying envelopes.

Avoid mailbox stuffing. Your first instinct will be to walk around your neighborhood and stuff your letters in your neighbors' mailboxes.

Unfortunately, it is a federal offense to insert letters into your neighbors' mailboxes. The post office likes you to pay for postage. There is a stiff fine to be paid as a penalty for stuffing mailboxes. One mail carrier assured me that a jail sentence could also be imposed on mailbox stuffers.

In reality, a peeved mail carrier may remove your letters from mailboxes and simply give you a warning telephone call to alert you to the fact that your letters were illegally distributed. He will tell you not to do it again. And that's that.

Frankly, many mail carriers will not mind at all if they see your letters. They will leave them untouched in the mailboxes and not think twice about it. But you are just beginning an organization. So it is probably best to start without risking a federal offense. Try to resist the natural temptation to stuff mailboxes.

If you live in a rural neighborhood, simply drive up to your neighbors' homes and ring the bell to talk to them, handing them your letter in person. However, rural homes often present dogs and fences as obstacles. The front door may be inaccessible. No need to risk life and limb. In case of a locked gate or snarling dog, leave your letter in the newspaper slot near the street mailbox or rolled up and inserted into the fence.

If you live in a suburban neighborhood, it is easy to walk the streets and place your letters partially under your neighbors' front doormats or doorjambs (so that they will not blow away) or in newspaper funnels. If you have the time, knock on doors to talk personally with your neighbors about your concerns as you hand out the letters.

Apartment and condominium complexes demand different approaches. One method is to tape your letter to the mailbox area, perhaps on the outside of the magazine slot. Insert extra copies into the magazine slot for people to take. If the mailboxes are locked inside the building, then slide copies of your letter under the front door or under the mat. Not everyone in the building will see your letter this way. Eventually, the manager will dispose of most copies in an attempt to keep the front hall neat. But all you need is to reach one receptive person per building. Then, in the future, that person can easily notify everyone else in the building about your budding organization.

It is also useful to attach copies of your letter to bulletin boards found in neighborhood cafes, laundromats, shops, and the post office.

You may also mail your "Dear Neighbor" letter to your local newspaper for the letters-to-the-editor page. This is an excellent idea because your letter will receive a citywide audience—for free.

Mailing is a last resort at this stage. You may still be a one-person or two-person organization, and mailings can be costly. Unless the money is no concern for you, wait until you have at least a small organization before using mailings, which are discussed in Chapter Three.

Your Organization's First Meeting

How many people should you invite to your first meeting? The number depends on how many people respond to your "Dear Neighbor" letter. Ten people at an initial meeting is plenty. At this early stage, you do not necessarily want a crowd. Therefore, don't be discouraged if only five to ten people respond to your letter. Later your organization may grow to several hundred or several thousand people. But you will notice throughout your years of growth that most of the organization's work will continue to be done by a few energetic people.

What if you receive dozens of telephone calls in response to your letter? Then, by all means, invite all enthusiastic callers to your first meeting.

Where to hold your first meeting? If you don't mind inviting strangers into your living room, then you can hold the meeting in your own home. However, if you wish to guard your living room as a bastion of privacy, or if you have toddlers playing underfoot, or if your spouse has to get to bed early every night, or if you have twelve indoor-dwelling cats, then simply ask one of your callers if it's okay to hold the initial meeting at his house.

What if you expect a crowd? If the response to your "Dear

Neighbor" letter is overwhelming and you expect a crowd, then contact city hall for a list of available public meeting rooms. Schools, banks, hospitals, churches, fire stations, and community centers often offer free meeting rooms for public use.

Wherever your meeting occurs, have someone sit at a table by the front door to greet all arrivals with a sign-up sheet requesting the person's name, address, and telephone number. This friendly greeting makes everyone feel welcome. Plus, the sign-up sheet will provide you with a valuable list for future contacts.

What should you hope to accomplish at your first meeting? This first meeting will be emotionally charged. You are a group of people under attack. You are about to fight for your values, for your community, for the environment. Study this group of people well. They may become your closest allies and friends. You are bound together in a grassroots struggle for victory. You need each other. This need will create lifelong bonds.

Let's say that your group begins with ten neighbors in your living room. It is a good time to assess the ten people you invited. Who is the most articulate? Who understands how your local government works? Who has contacts on the city council? Who knows any facts about the developer? Who belongs to environmental organizations? Who naturally takes the leadership role? Who are the most eager to volunteer their time?

During this first meeting, if you have fewer than twenty-five people present, go around the room to let people introduce themselves one by one to the group. People give their names and where they live. Find out who belongs to environmental, political, civic, or other organizations.

Someone should take the lead to run the meeting. That someone usually is the person who wrote the "Dear Neighbor" letter. Let's say that person is you. Begin discussion of your community problem. Outline what you know about the development that threatens you all. Then give everyone a chance to express what they know about the development, the developer, and the political climate of your town. People will need to vent their fear and anger.

Your first meeting should accomplish one important task: to initiate the search for mentors and information. Several people should leave the meeting with the assignment of talking to someone who might have information about the development.

Volunteers should seek out local officials. One person should volunteer to contact the planning department to talk with a planner about the development project. Someone else should telephone city hall to try to find out which city council members might be the most supportive of your position. You will be surprised; even the secretary who answers the city hall telephone can give you some useful information if plied with questions. Another volunteer should call the county supervisor's office. Find out who your supervisor is and what she or he stands for. Is your supervisor a friend of developers and oil companies? Or is your supervisor an avid hiker and bird watcher?

Other volunteers should seek out your local environmental organizations and attend their meetings. Your local reference librarian will be able to help you find a list of all the conservation organizations in your area. Or, if you contact one conservation group, such as your local Sierra Club or Audubon Society chapter, that organization is likely to have a list of most of the other environmental groups in your area.

Also ask someone to contact your local housing associations, meet with their presidents for coffee, and attend one of their meetings. Explain to these housing associations that you are creating an organization to preserve the quality of life in your area and you need their help.

In your forays to various environmental, housing, and political organizations, you will encounter a handful of people who will prove exceptionally helpful and supportive. These people will become your mentors. Invite these individuals out for coffee one by one. Ask them every question you can think of. Dedicated activists are always looking for fresh enthusiasts to help environmental causes. So don't be shy. Almost every environmental activist you contact will be happy to meet with you and answer your questions.

What should you ask your mentors? Take along plenty of paper and a pen to your meetings with your new activist mentors. Take voluminous notes on their advice. Key questions to ask them are:

- What do your mentors know about the developer and the development?

- Which people in local political offices are likely to be supportive of your organization's position?

- Which politicians and organizations are likely to oppose your group?

- What do your mentors advise you and your budding organization to do, step by step?

- Whom else do your mentors recommend you to contact for further information and advice?

If you telephone and meet with every person your mentors recommend, you will soon develop a chain of important personal contacts and allies whom you will be able to count on for future advice and help. In addition, you will have learned a tremendous amount about local government in a short, but intense, period of time.

This period in your life will provide a high learning curve. Your search for information will be the equivalent of a crash course on how democracy works at a local level. There are few things as exciting!

Most importantly, you will learn that experienced activists exist in your community who are eager and willing to help you. Furthermore, you will be relieved to learn that our political system will permit you to organize to try to make this a better world. But not without a fight!

Your Organization's Next Meetings

After two to three weeks of networking, your group should meet again to pool the names and information you gathered in your hectic weeks of coffees and meetings. You will be amazed how much you have learned in such a short time.

These early information-gathering meetings may be limited to those in your group who volunteered to seek out mentors. With such initiative, these people are likely to be the future leaders of your organization.

After pooling your information, decide among you who are your most useful and reliable mentors and who are the most sympathetic local leaders. Plan to invite one or two of these people to your next meeting. To encourage personal bonds, have the person who originally met with a particular mentor invite that mentor to be the guest speaker at your meeting.

This next meeting should be a big one. The time has come to invite additional neighbors and friends who may not have replied to the original "Dear Neighbor" letter but who might be interested in the issue. Now that your group is better informed, it's time to start building up the numbers of your new organization.

For your first expanded meeting, you could simply have members of your core group invite several of their friends and neighbors. However, if you feel ready for a bigger turnout, then distribute a leaflet announcing the big meeting. List the date, time, location, and purpose of the meeting, along with the names and titles of the speakers, plus the name and telephone number of the contact person within your budding organization for callers who need further information. Following is an example of such a leaflet.

Dear Friends and Neighbors:

The city is considering a plan to fill the one thousand acres of marshland on the edge of town in order to build a new shopping center. We feel that our marshlands with their abundant wildlife are more important than yet another shopping mall.

We have invited several experts to address the community on this vital issue. Come join us. Bring your friends and neighbors.

EVENT: Community Meeting on Marshland Preservation
PLACE: Hometown High School Auditorium
TIME: July 10, 8:00 P.M.
SPEAKERS: Wanda Wetland, Wildlife Alliance
　　　　　　Phil Birdwell, Environmental League
　　　　　　Frank Fishfinn, Conservation Corps

The event is free and the public is welcome.

For further information, contact Ed Egret at 222-2222.

If your group seeks maximum attendance, then send this announcement to your local newspaper and request that it be listed as an upcoming event. Also mail the announcement to the press in the form of a letter to the editor to be printed on the editorial page. If you desire even more press attention, then invite your local newspaper editor and reporters to attend the meeting.

At this early stage, a large meeting with high attendance and good press coverage will catapult your group into the public eye. Through press coverage you will garner more members quickly and also educate the public on the problem your group is addressing.

A large public meeting will also attract your opposition. For example, in the case of the Marshland Preservation meeting, proponents of the shopping mall are likely to attend with their rhetoric on how a shopping center would boost the town's finances, bring in revenue dollars, and provide jobs. Besides, who needs the muddy old marshes anyway? The slimy ooze just breeds mosquitoes!

Be aware of the risk that at a large public meeting your opposition may have organized to outnumber your wetlands supporters. Your meeting could be completely disrupted and taken over by the opposition.

Decide whether your group is ready for such a confrontation. At some point you will be ready, but perhaps not just yet. That's why an invitation-only meeting of your immediate neighbors and friends may obtain even better results at this early stage of your organization.

If the invited speakers are told in advance that they are to address twenty concerned community members in your living room, then that is what they will expect to address. Don't feel obliged to provide an enormous audience for the speakers. Many local politicians and environmental activists are happy to address a group of any size.

When should you hold meetings? For maximum attendance, begin your meetings at seven-thirty or eight o'clock in the evening. This gives people time to commute home from work and at least gulp down a hasty dinner.

Larger meetings should be held Monday through Thursday evenings. Avoid weekend meetings. People often have other plans on the weekends. Don't force your members to choose between a meeting and a weekend camping trip. The camping trip will usually win.

Tips for a Successful Meeting

A successful meeting informs your members and inspires them to dedication to your environmental cause. Every meeting is a call to action. Here are the basics for a productive meeting:

- Have a sign-up sheet at a welcome table by the front door for each person to write in his or her name, address, and telephone number before the meeting. Have someone friendly sitting at the welcome table to gather the names. Provide name tags.

- Begin and end the meeting on time. Don't exhaust people with long, drawn-out meetings.

- Keep the meeting interesting, invigorating, and high-spirited.

- List the agenda at the beginning of the meeting. State clearly what the purpose of the meeting is. List the order in which various items will be discussed. Introduce yourself, key organizers of your group, and your guest speakers.

- Give people at the meeting a feeling of belonging. Present the issues in such a way that people feel personally threatened by the development and personally benefited by being active in your group. People tend to be involved as much as they feel they have something close to their hearts at stake, such as their health, their property values, their quality of life, their children's safety, etc.

- Let people express their questions and concerns.

- Be certain that the meeting accomplishes its purpose.

- Keep the meeting on track. Minimize digressions. If the meeting goes off on a tangent, simply break in to say, "Remember, our purpose here is to . . . Let's get back to the issue."

- Use visual aids, such as maps of the affected area and a chalkboard with a list of issues and the agenda. If you lack a chalkboard, use a large piece of paper with the items written in bold lettering. Display this list throughout the meeting.

- If arguments break out and your group cannot reach a consensus, you can do one of several things. First, point out that you are in a deadlock. Then ask the group if you should table the discussion until a future meeting. Or present the option of putting the issue up for a vote. Or let the debate continue until the issue resolves itself.

- At the end of the meeting, state briefly the accomplishments of the meeting, thank everyone for coming, and announce that you look forward to seeing everyone at the next meeting.

Your First Meeting with a Decision Maker

After your group has met with a few mentors, such as environmental activists, housing association leaders, and public officials who may be on your side, it's time to invite a decision maker to one of your meetings. This bigwig may be the mayor, a city council member, or a county supervisor. Let's say that your group chooses to invite your city's mayor to a meeting with twenty of your concerned neighbors in your living room.

Before your meeting with Mayor Bigwig, visit your local planning department to pick up any information on file regarding Mr. Pillar-of-Society's development proposal. Let's say you live on Pastoral Lane and are opposing the gigantic new development. A master plan for that project may already be on file. If so, pick up a few copies, which may cost a few dollars each. Distribute these copies to the most astute members of your new group. At least a few of you should plough through the master plan's tedious pages before your meeting with the mayor. A master plan gives a detailed description of a proposal, including architectural sketches, property lines, zoning information, hills that will be sliced off, trees that will be cut down, creeks that will be dammed, etc. Master plans are prepared by the developer's consultants, so they tend to downplay the destructive side of the project.

You may not be able to make heads or tails of the master plan. Don't worry. You'll probably have months to study every painful detail. But for now, just prepare a list of questions to ask the mayor and the city planner, whom the mayor is likely to bring along to the meeting.

This meeting with the mayor will be your official plunge into shark-infested political waters. Hang on for the ride of your life! Study the mayor well. From the mayor's point of view, your group may be just twenty disgruntled, confused people, a bunch of nobodies. You may not even have an organizational name yet. The mayor will probably be cordial out of professional protocol. Because you are not yet a political force, don't expect him to be overly concerned with your point of view. You are not a power in the community. Not yet. But soon you will be.

So, twenty of your neighbors are seated around your living room, eating cookies, and waiting to hear what the mayor has to say. Let's imagine the worst scenario. The mayor is clearly a friend of the developer. The mayor describes Mr. Pillar-of-Society in glowing terms. They belong to the same church and the same bridge club. They play golf together. Mr. Pillar-of-Society surely wants only the best for the community. Don't we need a new hospital and fire station? Don't we need more housing? After all, housing promotes jobs. Consider the added revenue this development will bring to our town! But, you object, this is a peaceful little street with no problems at all. Won't a monstrously huge project completely destroy Pastoral Lane?

"Well," responds the mayor, "that's progress."

Gagging on your cookies, you're all thinking, "Oh no, we haven't got a chance!"

But you do. Mayor is an elected position. You can vote this fellow out of office. Moreover, you can run your own candidates against him.

By now, you will begin a list in your own mind, soon to be put on paper. The list has three headings: Allies, Enemies, and Go-betweens. Place the mayor at the top of your "Enemies" heading (just under Mr. Pillar-of-Society). There is no need to tell him this, of course. By all means, thank the mayor for coming. Continue asking questions. Pump him for all the information you can squeeze out of him. Just beneath his surface cordiality, the mayor may be contemptuous of your little band of upstarts who think they have the right to complain about his rich friend's project. This contempt, this underestimating of your potential power, will be his undoing. If he does not take you seriously, then he won't be prepared for your political assault. All the better for you.

After all your questions have been answered (or avoided), graciously show the mayor and the planner to the door. No need making explicit enemies just yet. Stay polite. After the mayor has left, discuss with your group what your next step should be.

Now let's imagine a different scenario. Your mayor walks in with the city planner and turns out to be a moderate. Madam Mayor tells you, "Mr. Pillar-of-Society? No, I've never met the man, though I have heard about him. His project? Well, our city sure does need a new hospital. But then isn't this area zoned only for low-density housing with agricultural uses?" The mayor checks with the planner on this, and the planner nods. "You can't just rezone a whole neighborhood without lots of consideration!" she continues. "This needs some looking into."

Bravo! You're lucky enough to have a moderate mayor. This is someone to befriend, to take out for coffee, to call by her first name. Moderates are by definition middle of the road. They can be swayed. It's your organization's job to sway her. But you can be certain that Mr. Pillar-of-Society will be inviting her out for lunch and to his country club for dinner with his family (he has five adorable children and a lovely wife).

Here's a third scenario. It's rare, but not impossible. Your mayor is for slow growth. Not only that, he's an environmentalist. Now, don't scoff in disbelief! It is possible. This mayor will listen patiently to your concerns for a while, then interrupt you. (Every politician, even an environmentalist, can't sit without talking for long. It's a biological need of the political species.) This mayor says, "Mr. Pillar-of-Society's project is an abomination. He can't just waltz into your neighborhood and completely transform it. He has no right to ask you to give up your way of life. And what about the traffic, the pollution, the noise?" You think you're dreaming. This guy actually cares. He actually understands.

But your worries are not over. Even good mayors who believe in environmental integrity can lose elections. Your new ally may be out of office by the time Mr. Pillar-of-Society's development comes before the city council for a vote. Furthermore, your good mayor may be in a minority position on the city council. Perhaps four out of the five city council members are in favor of big development.

What you are now encountering is the great game of local

government—a serious game that you plan on winning. You must get to know the players, their strengths and weaknesses, their allies, and their enemies. The local players are Mr. Pillar-of-Society, his allies, the mayor, the city council members, the county supervisors, the city planner, local newspapers, environmental organizations, and, most importantly, you and your neighbors.

At some time in the future, depending on the nature of the project, you may need the help of federal and state agencies and politicians, such as the Environmental Protection Agency, the Army Corps of Engineers, the Department of Fish and Game, and your senators and congressional representatives. However, the primary grassroots confrontations occur right in your own hometown with your own local officials.

Goals of Your First Meeting with a Decision Maker

Your initial meeting with the mayor, city council member, or county supervisor lets that decision maker know that you exist as a neighborhood and that you're angry, scared, and organizing to fight the development and to protect the environment. That in itself is a lot.

You'll need to become familiar with the planning process, so pump the mayor, the city planner, and other officials for information about the planning process so that you know what your next move should be. Key questions are:

- What does the planning process include? Is an Environmental Impact Report required? Are any other reports or studies required on the project? By whom?

- What commissions or organizations must approve the project before it can proceed? Your group will eventually contact, in writing or in person, every commission involved.

- When are public hearings going to be held on the project? Your organization must be prepared to make impressive presentations at every upcoming public hearing.

Ask the mayor and the planner to notify your organization of all aspects of this project, especially all public hearings. Make sure that the mayor and planner leave with the name, address, and telephone number of one member of your group as a future contact. Follow up on this request with a written letter thanking the mayor for coming and reiterating your contact's name and your request to be notified about all phases of the project. What if your mayor ignores your request? Simply continue to repeat this request to the mayor, his or her staff, and the planning department by telephone and letters until they start complying. Also, make certain that your organization's contact person is listed with both city and county staffs, as these bureaucracies usually maintain separate mailing lists.

During your meeting, study how the individuals in your group react to the mayor. Who asks bold questions? Who seems to know something about the planning process? Who hits it off best with the mayor? Identify people in your organization who will make the best liaisons with your mayor, supervisors, council members, and planners. A personal, congenial rapport between individuals in your group and public officials is an extremely powerful political tool.

As your meeting comes to a close, you will have discovered some of your group's strengths. As people entered the meeting at the front door, everyone signed in on a sheet of paper, listing name, address, and telephone number. Before the meeting is over, make sure that you connect the names and faces of the most impressive people in your group. They are likely to become your future steering committee (discussed in Chapter Two). If one of your neighbors is particularly rude or disruptive, make note of his name also. You may want to leave him out of future smaller meetings, although he might be effective at large city council meetings when a little yelling and screaming can go a long way to waking up the council members.

Congratulations! You have taken the first steps toward controlling your own destiny and becoming a power in your community. With all the challenges that grassroots political activism entails, it will also provide you with an intense, exciting, rewarding period in your life. You are taking actions to determine the destiny of your community. It will change your life in wonderful ways that you cannot even imagine now. Your battles will forge lifelong friendships. Your victories will give you unforeseen power and respect in your community.

As the saying goes, "If the people will lead, the leaders will eventually follow." So lead on!

CHAPTER 2

Leadership and Teamwork

T he time has come to give internal structure to your organization. Every organization evolves at its own unique pace, so don't feel pressured to select a name or elect officers too soon. The members of some newborn organizations believe that the urgency of information gathering and networking outweighs the needs of establishing a bureaucratic structure. Such a group may wait weeks or months before choosing a name for their organization or thinking about the election of officers.

Other organizations feel more comfortable setting up an immediate hierarchy of officers and committees. Decide among your own core group of volunteers the best time for you to begin structuring your organization.

Your group may not care much for official titles. Perhaps you are just neighbors trying to preserve your community on one particular issue. No matter how loosely knit you would like to remain, you will find that politicians, public officials, governmental agencies, and other organizations expect a certain traditional structure. They expect you to elect a president who is your principal spokesperson, as well as a body of decision-making officers. They expect a bona fide organizational name. Plus, they respect large membership numbers and impressive newsletters.

Those of you freewheeling activists who don't give a hoot for fancy titles or bylaws will at least have to pay lip service to such structural demands in order to gain credibility in your community.

To become an effective organization, you do need to choose a name, elect officers, write up bylaws, collect dues, create committees, and meet on a regular basis. However, my advice to you is to spend as little time as possible on bureaucratic trivia. Always remember that your goal is to protect and enhance your environment, to fight the good fight, to win your political battles. An organization that wastes too much time on bureaucratic nonsense will lose its vitality, make no impact on the community, and go the way of the dinosaur.

View internal organizational matters as the skeletal structure of your group, a solid base on which to develop your political muscle.

Formalizing Your Organization

Choosing a Name

When it's time to choose a name for your organization, ask everyone in your core group for suggestions. Be creative. Mull over the possibilities together. Think of all the pros and cons of every suggestion. Don't settle on a name until you come up with one with plenty of pros and no cons. Take the time to do it right, and keep in mind the following:

- The name should be able to grow with the organization. So consider your long-term goals. You will have to live with this name for years to come.

- Make sure the name is easy to say and easy to remember.

- Create a name that can be reduced to a catchy acronym. Here are a few examples: SOS (Save Our Seashore), WONT (Women Opposed to Nuclear Technology), ACORN (Association of Community Organizations for Reform Now), BLAST (Bring Legal Action to Stop Tanks), TEACH (Tennesseans Against Chemical Hazards).

- The name should reflect your membership and your purpose.

- Be careful not to make the name so restrictive that it turns off potential members. For example, housing associations sometimes make the mistake of calling themselves homeowners' associations, thereby turning away all the renters in a neighborhood who would like to become involved.

- Avoid choosing a name that is so similar to another organization's name that the two groups can be easily mistaken for each other.

Once your organization has a name, it is time to shout it from the rooftops. Notify your city and county administrations of your organization's name and mailing address. You can use the home address of your president (see below) or you may want to rent a post office box for your organization so that as your president changes from year to year, your organization's mailing address remains constant. Let the city and county planning departments know that you want to be on their mailing lists and expect to be notified about all city and county activities and projects affecting your group.

This is also the time to write a letter to the editor for the editorial page of your local newspapers announcing the creation of your organization. Explain your organization's purpose and give a contact number for people to call if they want to get involved. You can also send an amended version of this letter as a press release to local newspaper editors themselves to encourage them to do an article on your organization and its goals.

Bylaws and Rules of Order

Your organization is going to need bylaws to set structural parameters for your group. Bylaws cover rules for elections, membership, dues, general meetings, decision making, etc. Have your treasurer or secretary (see below) contact other neighborhood organizations or local environmental groups for copies of their bylaws. Model your bylaws on theirs where appropriate. There is no need to reinvent the wheel. Simply delete or add whatever provisions to suit the bylaws to your own needs. The bylaws can be as simple or complex as you want to make them. Do yourself a favor and keep the bylaws simple! Above all, don't make your bylaws so restrictive that they actually impede effective action.

The next step is to go to your local library to check out *Robert's Rules of Order,* which is the standard guide for how to run an orderly meeting. This guide explains such things as how to pass a motion, recognize speakers from the floor, etc. It is particularly useful for large meetings. Make certain that your officers are familiar with *Robert's Rules of Order,* though you need not follow it to the letter. Adapt it to your needs. Your group may naturally function at a much more casual level, which is fine.

Nonprofit Status and Incorporation

Your group can function perfectly well as an organization without nonprofit status and without incorporating. You, as a group, must decide which works best for you.

Incorporation has the advantage of protecting the officers of your group in the event of a lawsuit. Without a corporate structure to protect your organization, the individual leaders of your group could be held personally liable in a lawsuit. A few hours of legal work in order to incorporate your organization could save your leadership from such risks.

Nonprofit status offers certain financial benefits, such as reduced postage rates. However, it does include certain restrictions, such as limiting your group's political involvement in elections. Nonetheless, individuals within your group remain free to participate in elections in any way that they wish. Besides, during an election, a separate organization can be created to endorse and campaign for candidates.

Contact your local conservation groups and housing associations to ask their opinions on incorporation and nonprofit status. Also write away for free catalogues of books available from Nolo Press, Island Press, and Sierra Club Books. These publishers provide excellent guides on legal issues for environmental organizations.

For further legal advice, the Environmental Defense Fund, the Sierra Club Legal Defense Fund, and the Natural Resources Defense Council provide expertise in all environmental matters. Their addresses and phone numbers are provided in the appendix.

Electing Officers

Your first election of officers is likely to occur within your small core group of volunteers. After all, your new organization may not have much of a membership yet. After the first year, your organization should allow the entire membership an opportunity to vote for officers. But that first election is different.

At the beginning, you are likely to be a handful of dedicated volunteers eager to get the job done and not overly concerned with titles. So try to divide up the positions according to abilities. For example, your organization's core group may consist of six people. You can assign volunteers an appropriate title that suits them. In addition to the four elected positions—president, vice-president, treasurer, and secretary—add the assigned titles of newsletter editor and communications committee chair.

There is always plenty of work to go around, so feel free to create titles to cover everyone and every task so that no one in your initial core group feels left out. Other titles might include: press secretary, for the person who is in charge of writing your organization's press releases and notifying newspapers about all your events; meeting coordinator, for the person who reserves the locations for your meetings, makes sure that there are enough chairs, a podium, a microphone, coffee and cookies, a sign-in desk, etc.; letters-to-the-editor coordinator, for the person responsible for keeping a flow of letters to the editor to your local newspapers on the hot issues that concern you; and membership coordinator, for the person who oversees that your growing membership mailing list is complete, accurate, and up-to-date.

If you have a large core group of volunteers, make everyone feel useful. Give everyone some specific task.

If you start out with a small core group of four people, let's say, then everyone has the honor of being an officer: president, vice-president, secretary, or treasurer. These four leaders may do all the initial organizational work, but this is not a problem. Bigger is not necessarily better. Four hard-working activists with a cooperative spirit can accomplish environmental and political miracles by creating an influential organization.

President

The president of your organization is your principal contact with the public. To the rest of the world, he or she speaks for your organization. Your president is the person whom the developer, the mayor, the supervisors, and the local newspapers will contact. The president runs your meetings and determines the agenda. To the community, this person represents the face and voice of your organization.

Good traits for a president are:

• *Coolness under fire.*   Many confrontations await your organization. Your president should be someone who can deal calmly with confrontation. In the heat of battle, he should be someone who knows how to listen and learn, rather than someone who spouts off whenever emotions overwhelm him. He should be someone who can funnel his anger into articulate expression without shouting or name-calling. He should also be diplomatic enough to be able to meet your adversaries and negotiate calmly but firmly. Your president should be able to stick by your organization's positions, no matter how compelling or insistent the opposition. He should feel comfortable lunching with the mayor, meeting with the county supervisors, negotiating with developers, and giving interviews with the press.

For example, the person with whom I cofounded an activist organization was a tall, lanky computer wizard who also happened to be an expert card player. His poker face and ever-ready calm under fire taught me volumes about dealing with the opposition. Every confrontation with your adversary demands a poker player's steely nerves.

• *The ability to delegate, delegate, delegate.*   The president should be a good judge of character so that she can delegate tasks to the appropriate people. She should be someone willing and able to share power. You don't want a petty dictator taking over your organization.

• *Efficiency.*   The president should run a tight meeting. Digressions can run rampant at meetings. After all, you live in the same area, your children may go to the same schools, you may have the same favorite restaurants. So it is tempting to chat about these other matters during your meetings. In fact, some light banter is useful to add levity to serious meetings. It also bonds friendships. But the president must keep your meetings on track. People tire of coming to too many meetings or to meetings that last too late into the evening. So you must accomplish the maximum at each meeting.

Vice-president
The main trait of a good vice-president is the ability to work well with the president. They will be attending many meetings together. They will spend lots of time conferring on the telephone. They must get along well.

As a safety precaution, whenever there is a meeting with your opposition or any public official (in his office or even for coffee), at least two of your organization's representatives should go along in case of disputes or "memory lapses." You will be amazed how many people will promise you one thing in private, then do the complete opposite in public. It is important to have more than one witness to back up your claims of what the opposition or a politician actually did promise (or threaten).

Your representatives at these small meetings will often be your president and vice-president. They must have their cues synchronized. They should not contradict each other in the presence of your opposition. They should be a solid team.

Many United States presidents choose vice-presidents who are ceremonial, whose main task is shaking hands and kissing babies. To the contrary, your vice-president must be hardworking.

Treasurer
The treasurer must be meticulous and scrupulous. It is the treasurer's job to keep your organization's bank account, to collect and record the dues. She must be honest and very well organized. The treasurer should provide regular updated reports on your organization's finances at your meetings.

One organization to which I belonged had a perfect treasurer with just the right traits for the job. He was someone who loved collecting things and filed and stored all the organization's paperwork for years. He was obsessively neat. Even his garage was immaculately clean! He actually looked forward to bank statements!

It is a good fundraising idea to place your treasurer at the welcome table by the front door at your large meetings. He can collect dues, renew memberships, and graciously accept donations as people sign in. Your treasurer should be someone who enjoys collecting money for a worthy cause.

Secretary

Keep the secretary's job simple. There is no need to create unnecessary paperwork. The secretary need not scribble down every word spoken at your meetings. A few brief paragraphs summing up the decisions made at your meetings are more than sufficient. These meeting summaries should be kept in a notebook. The same notebook can be passed from secretary to secretary over the years.

On the other hand, it is common among many organizations to demand that the secretary type up the minutes of every meeting and then mail these minutes to the leaders of the organization for their perusal. At each meeting, it is often the first item on the agenda to amend and approve the minutes of the previous meeting. This process creates an accurate record of all meetings and key decisions.

It is up to your group to decide how important these minutes are and whether it is necessary to have the secretary type them, mail them, and then amend them. After all, there are some very effective, rough-and-ready activist groups that take no minutes whatsoever.

So decide among yourselves the role that your secretary should play. Let the secretary's job remain flexible so that it may grow with your organization's needs.

Creating Committees

Communications Committee

The communications committee is the lifeline to your membership and the most important committee your organization will ever form.

The most vital role of the communications committee is to maintain the telephone tree. The communications committee chair creates a telephone tree. She prepares a list of ten or more reliable volunteers. Each of these ten volunteers in turn has a list of ten to twenty people to call. Therefore, whenever you need a large turnout at a public meeting, the communications chair calls her ten committee members, who in turn do their calling to notify your membership of the crucial meeting. Telephoning is by far the fastest and cheapest way to spread the word about upcoming events. It also is the most effective way to assure a large turnout.

Make no mistake about it. In the game of politics, numbers talk. It is impossible to overstate the importance of generating large crowds of people at any public hearing regarding your cause. Yet sometimes your local government may give your president only seven days' notice before a vitally important public hearing. In such cases, there is often no time for your organization to mail out notices to your membership. Without a communications committee you are lost. Yet with a well-organized telephone tree, your group can notify hundreds of people within a twenty-four to forty-eight hour period.

The telephone tree callers explain to your members where the meeting is, what it is about, and the urgency of attending. They can answer your members' questions. Once your members are notified and well informed, turnout is sure to be high. No matter what the crisis, your group is ready to mobilize quickly.

The second key role of the communications committee is to assemble the mail crew. The mail crew meets to stuff envelopes, lick stamps, and apply address labels to mail out your newsletters and notices. Always make these mail crew sessions fun. Order pizza and drinks. Put on some lively music. Crack jokes. The more tedious the work, the more volunteers deserve rewards. And stuffing envelopes is tedious! Yet, if you keep the mail crew sessions enjoyable, all the volunteers will be eager to return for the next mailing.

Even if you have the time to mail out notices to your membership about a meeting, if your communications committee gives everyone a reminder call in addition to the mailing, you are likely to double the attendance at the meeting. Nothing brings out people to a meeting like a telephone call from a concerned neighbor. Make your reminder calls two to three days before a public hearing to stress its urgency.

Within your communications committee, you can assign block or district captains. If your organization has grown to a membership of hundreds or even thousands of people, then dividing your city into districts is a manageable way of keeping communications vibrant and efficient. Each district captain, on short notice, can muster district volunteers to leaflet homes in his or her assigned district or make telephone calls to the residents of this area.

By assigning districts, no single volunteer is overwhelmed with too many people to contact. You never want to overburden any volunteer with more than he or she can handle. Burnout quickly drains enthusiasm, and your organization may lose a valuable volunteer.

A note on good communications committee chairs: good communications committee chairs come in all shapes and sizes. In New Hampshire, one organization's first chair was a soft-spoken fireman who was recovering from a back injury that kept him at home. He was extremely dedicated, and when he eventually moved to Arizona for his health, he soon was elected to an important public office in his new hometown because he had learned so much about local politics from his communications committee post.

Another communications committee chair was a homemaker tied to her many children's demands. Her home life never left her free to attend evening meetings, but she contributed greatly to her organization by telephoning others to make sure that they did attend the meetings.

Yet another communications chair was a dynamic woman who spent hours weekly on the telephone informing the community about vital issues. An outgoing "people person," she also often took it upon herself to go door to door to talk face to face with neighbors.

Communication is the key to building and maintaining an effective organization. Farm-worker organizer Cesar Chavez was once asked by young organizers for the recipe for successful organizing. Chavez replied: "Well, first you talk to one person, then another person, then you talk to another person . . ." That sums it up nicely.

Steering Committee

The steering committee is the core group of leaders in your organization. It consists of your officers, your committee chairs, your newsletter editor, plus other people willing to volunteer their time to be among the decision makers of your organization.

The steering committee meets on a regular basis to assess the evolution of your environmental issues and to determine what actions your organization needs to take—such as to decide how often the organization's newsletter appears, to select what articles to include in it, to discuss which public officials to contact, to write letters to agencies or commissions, to assign fact-finding missions, to organize fundraising events, to schedule large community meetings, to strategize for public hearings, and so on. If your environmental organization is deep in the midst of a heated controversy, then the steering committee may need to meet every week for a period of time in order to function effectively. But in an ongoing organization, monthly meetings are usually adequate to deal with all the issues.

Steering committees may be small and consist of merely the officers and the committee chairs, or may grow to a dozen or more people. The problem with a small steering committee is that too much work falls on too few shoulders. This can lead to burnout and exhaustion. The danger of too many steering committee members is that the decision-making process becomes unwieldy. Find the happy medium for your group. A small steering committee can be just as effective as a large one if the individuals involved are willing to do a lot of work.

Teamwork Is the Key to Success

Good teamwork will determine the success of your organization. Following are some keys to good teamwork.

Internal Debate, External Unity

Encourage debate within the steering committee. A vital steering committee will be loaded with strong personalities who agree and disagree on a number of issues. Debate and discussion are useful methods of examining all sides of an issue. If someone on the steering committee disagrees with everyone else, then it behooves everyone else to try to convince that person. Use reason, not shouting and name-calling. If the person remains unconvinced, then she should still be willing to go along with the steering committee's majority opinion. Everyone on the steering committee should invite debate, but should always be willing to yield to the majority.

Although debate should be strongly encouraged within your steering committee inner sanctum, your opposition should see your organization as a unified force. Never let on to the outside world about any dissension or division in your organization. Your opposition will see this as weakness and take advantage of it. Your leadership will lose credibility to the outside world if the rumor spreads that dissension is dividing your organization. Always resolve your differences within the walls of your steering committee meetings.

Dealing with Dissension

How do you deal with serious dissension within your organization? You have a number of options.

If you do not like the direction your organization's leaders are taking, one alternative is to resign from the organization in protest. You can begin another organization. The great environmentalist David Brower did this with marked success. He served as the Sierra Club's first executive director for many years. When the Sierra Club, for a brief period, was not as outspoken against nuclear power as Brower wished, he began Friends of the Earth to create connections between peace and environmental issues. Eventually Friends of the Earth chose to relocate from the San Francisco area to Washington, D.C. However, Brower decided to remain in the San Francisco area to form Earth Island Institute, along with many other subsequent organizations and projects. Meanwhile Brower and the Sierra

Club soon resolved most of their differences, and he returned as one of its prominent leaders.

Another alternative is *not* to resign, but to hang in there and try to turn the organization around to your way of thinking.

For example, a local environmental group was growing too moderate. They were making many compromises with the business community in order to get local businesses involved in environmental issues. Gradually, the environmental group seemed to have sold out completely. Their board of directors became watered down with nonenvironmentalists who compromised its powers away.

The reaction of some environmentalists was to resign in disgust, but others did not resign. They tried to get the organization back on track. The group had once been an environmental power, buying up land to donate to the public trust. They believed it could be a strong environmental force once again.

It is the leadership that so often determines the philosophy of an organization. So try to change the leadership. Put people with your own vision back on the board of directors. Outnumber your internal opposition. This takes time. Be patient. Do not give up on an organization just because its leadership is temporarily off track. The life of every organization has its ups and downs.

Yet another option is to find a mediator. If your steering committee is deadlocked on a certain issue and no imminent agreement flickers on the horizon, consider a mediator. This person should be someone whom all sides respect, someone who has no stake in the decision at hand. The mediator encourages debate and cooperation as each side expresses its views and eventually comes to some compromise agreement.

Some organizations that are going through a protracted period of internal dissension on a number of issues wisely set up a mediation board to resolve these disagreements as quickly as possible.

No Loose Cannons

It is a cardinal rule that everyone on the steering committee act only after conferring with others on the steering committee.

This holds true for the president and for committee chairs as much as for anyone else. The president and committee chairs will frequently have a lot of minor decisions to make. A meeting need not be called to handle each of these minor decisions. However, it is essential that each decision be discussed with another steering committee member for approval. This also holds true for letters sent out on your organization's stationery. A quick telephone call to another steering committee member will usually deal effectively and efficiently with the matter.

This rule is necessary for two reasons: (1) it prevents loose cannons from shooting off their mouths in the name of your organization, spouting statements that could embarrass or discredit your group; and (2) it prevents oversights. No matter how savvy your president, it is likely that she or he won't see all aspects of every situation. Conferring with the vice-president or another steering committee member on decisions is a great way to avoid these oversights, which can be disastrous in the long run.

Always Outnumber Your Opposition

Whenever you meet with your opposition, you should try to have more people present on your side than on their side. For example, you are to meet with your city's mayor. You know the mayor is a friend of Mr. Pillar-of-Society. The mayor is likely to have someone else present—a secretary, city manager, or city planner, for example. Find out in advance exactly who will be at the meeting with the mayor; then the appropriate number of people from your organization should go along. Ideally, your numbers should equal or exceed the numbers of your opposition.

Never Let Your President Meet
Alone with Your Opposition

There are some very important reasons why your organization's president—or any other representative of your group—should not go alone to a meeting with your opposition.

• *You never want to give the impression that your group is a one-person organization.* Your group's leaders only have power and influence if they are believed to represent many supporters.

• *Your opposition can gang up on your president.* For example, let's say you are meeting with your county supervisor. As president, you go alone to your supervisor's office to discuss the project you oppose. You enter the supervisor's office to find not only the supervisor, but also his aid, a county planner, plus the developer and his lawyers. You have been set up. They intend to intimidate you. To prevent this horrible scenario, whenever you plan to attend a meeting, always inquire who else will be at the meeting. Plan to take along at least an equal number of allies to balance the numbers.

• *You want a witness there.* For example, you may be representing your group at a luncheon meeting with the developer and the mayor. The developer may offer you part of the profits of his development if you abandon your opposition to his project. This is a clear bribe. You want a witness there.

Another example: At a meeting with your county supervisor, she makes you certain promises. It will be harder for her to deny these promises at a future time if you have a witness there to confirm what she actually promised.

• *Two heads are better than one.* In a meeting with a politician in particular, it always helps to have at least two on your side. One of you may simply forget to bring up a point. Or perhaps one of you is having trouble convincing the politician of the importance of your concerns. Having a colleague there doubles your communication skills.

• *It helps to have two sets of ears.* After a meeting, it helps to have more than one view in analyzing what really went on there. In the political world, there are always several layers of reality.

• *By going to meetings in numbers, you avoid your opposition's attempts to divide and conquer your organization.*

Under the guise of friendly overtures, your opposition may very well attempt to meet one by one with your officers and other key leaders in your organization in attempts to create dissension.

For example, the developer may invite your president to meet for a casual coffee, just the two of them, to get acquainted in an informal way. Your president makes the mistake of going alone. Then afterward, the developer invites your vice-president to lunch and tells her that your president agreed to all kinds of compromises. Your vice-president is shocked and doesn't know what to say. If you let him, the developer can do this with every one of your group's leaders individually. Your organization's leaders will soon distrust one another. The result will be total havoc for your group. Always remember the simple maxim: There is safety in numbers.

This rule of caution does not apply to meetings with your allies. It is important to develop personal ties with politicians, influential citizens, and community leaders who are on your side. If you can develop close one-on-one friendships with these allies, so much the better. As friends, they will enrich your life personally. As political allies, they will fight side by side for your cause.

Teamwork at its best is pure bliss. The concert of people working together to achieve a worthwhile goal provides one of the greatest pleasures in life. Individuals develop new skills. Lifelong friendships are forged. The organization and its leaders gain respect, prestige, and influence. Most importantly, the quality of life in your community has been improved. You have taken responsibility for your own future and made it a better one. You have become a power. But don't let it go to your head!

CHAPTER 3

🌲

How to Write and Distribute a Newsletter

The primary purpose of a newsletter is to keep your organization's membership informed. The benefits of a knowledgeable membership are numerous. Informed members are ready and eager to participate in meetings and public hearings; they are aware of all the work that the organization's leaders are accomplishing and gladly pay their dues year after year; and they volunteer their time and money as the need arises for committee work or donations.

A secondary purpose of your newsletter is to inform politicians and the press of your activities. In addition to your members, important players in your community should be on your newsletter mailing list to receive complimentary copies; these leaders include city council members, county supervisors, significant public officials and administrators, city and county planning directors, local newspaper editors, and presidents of key environmental and housing organizations. Your newsletter will remind these community players that your organization not only still exists, but also is a growing power.

Does your organization really need a newsletter? Absolutely! Without one, your members have no idea what the organization is accomplishing. Members may assume that the

organization is not active and will not renew their membership. You also lose an effective way of recruiting new members. Worst of all, without a newsletter, the leadership grows increasingly out of touch with the community and loses the community's respect. A newsletter is vitally important.

How frequently should you send out your newsletter? Never go out of your way to create work for yourself or your organization. That includes your newsletter. There is no need to write more newsletters than are necessary for effective action. Even during a fierce environmental battle, you may need only four or six newsletters a year. If by some miracle your organization is having a peaceful year with few battles to fight, two newsletters per year may be more than ample just to keep your membership up-to-date for the times when battles do arise.

It is crucial to send out newsletters before important public meetings. Your newsletter will inform people about when and where to show up for the meetings and, equally important, educate them on the issues so that they know what points to raise at the meetings.

Of course, your organization may eventually become quite large and well known. At that point it behooves you to send out newsletters on a regular basis. Your members will expect it. It is up to your leadership to decide whether your newsletters should go out quarterly or monthly.

You'll need to designate someone as editor of your newsletter. For some people writing is a pleasure. For other folks, putting pen to paper is a torture akin to the medieval rack. Ask your new steering committee who would like to be the newsletter editor. You will not receive a deluge of volunteers. You will be lucky to find one volunteer with a little writing experience, at least someone who takes pleasure in putting thoughts on paper.

It is wise to see a writing sample before choosing your newsletter editor. You need a literate person—perhaps someone who likes writing letters to the editors of your local newspapers.

Your newsletter editor should have good grammar and spelling skills. She should also be skilled at honing down articles to their bare essentials. Your community will be bored by long-winded, bombastic articles. Your newsletter articles should be short, readable, and factual.

You may decide to have your newsletter editor write your entire newsletter. But, ideally, it is best to have members of your steering committee volunteer to write brief articles on the specific issues at hand. Give them a deadline to submit the articles to your editor. It is her job to pare down the articles so that they all fit in your newsletter. No matter how much your editor stresses to your committee that the articles should be brief, they will inevitably be too long. Your editor must be able to discern what facts are important to leave in and what items are expendable.

What Articles Should Be in Your Newsletter?

Together, the steering committee should decide what topics should be covered in your newsletter and then assign each article to the steering committee member who is most conversant with that particular issue. Your initial newsletter might contain the following:

• *A cover story with details of the project in which you are involved.*   You want to galvanize your neighbors into action, make them understand exactly how they will be affected personally. People become involved when they feel personally threatened or rewarded.

If you are opposing a project, avoid defamatory remarks of any kind. You may attack Mr. Pillar-of-Society's project. But *never* attack Mr. Pillar-of-Society personally. Some people love lawsuits. There has been a spate of developers suing community associations to keep them quiet. Don't let this keep you quiet! These are usually nuisance suits, nicknamed "slap suits," because the litigant has not sustained any real damages, just a "slap" in the face, so to speak. Those who use a "slap suit" as a method of intimidation know that they can't win the lawsuit. Every community has the legal right to oppose projects publicly. If you are attentive to your language in public and in print, then the chances are good that you should not have legal problems. You have every right to express your concerns about any project.

• *An article about your new organization and its plans and goals.*   Make this article an appeal for members. List your committees and explain their purposes. Alert people to the membership form (see below) on the back page. This article should be boxed in to draw special attention to it. Stress that only your community's involvement can save your neighborhood. Be blunt. This article could be entitled "Save Your Neighborhood! Join Our Organization Today!"

• *An article about your meetings with public officials and community leaders.*   Once again, avoid all derogatory remarks about any individual. There is no point in going out of your way to make enemies. You may quote what a public official actually said or what he actually did, but don't editorialize about what a filthy, lying scumbag he is. Phrase your comments so that your readers will be able to draw this conclusion on their own. This discretion necessitates enormous self-control at times.

On the other hand, give lots of praise to public officials who are clearly on your side. They deserve plenty of support and applause. Send your political allies a copy of the newsletter so that they observe for themselves how much you publicly appreciate their support.

• *Communications committee article.*   One short article should be an appeal for volunteers to serve on the vital communications committee. Explain what committee volunteers are expected to do. In the article, list the name and telephone number of the committee chair so that volunteers can contact the chair directly. Here is a sample:

WANTED: COMMUNICATIONS COMMITTEE VOLUNTEERS

Our association's communications committee needs your help. We want volunteers for the telephone tree. Volunteers will receive a list of ten to twenty members' names and telephone numbers. Your job is to call everyone on this short list before important city council meetings where it is crucial to demonstrate strong support for our cause. The telephone tree is our way to ensure large crowds at meetings, yet it will take very little of your time. You will be able to do the calling at your leisure from the comfort of your home. To volunteer, call the communications committee chair, Colleen, at 212-1212.

• *A membership form.*   A membership form should appear in your first newsletter and in every subsequent newsletter. Leave plenty of space for a person to fill in his or her name, address, and telephone number. Here is a sample:

MEMBERSHIP FORM

YES! I want to join the Hometown Conservation League.
Enclosed is my check for $10 for one year.

Name _____

Address _____

City _____ Zip _____

Telephone number _____

Please make check payable to Hometown
Conservation League and mail to:

P.O. Box 121, Hometown, USA

• *Annual dues.*   When it is time to collect annual dues, ask for the fee to be mailed back with the membership form. The check should be made out to your organization's name. Your treasurer will open a bank account for your organization.

Make the dues minimal to induce the maximum amount of people to join. For example, for years the Save the San Francisco Bay Association has charged only a $1 per year membership fee to encourage many people to join. Nevertheless, $10 per year is an amount most people who care about your cause will pay without thinking twice. You can always ask your membership for more money later if need be. So never make your initial dues prohibitively high.

There are myriad creative ways to collect money for your organization above and beyond dues—for example, parties, auctions, garage sales, flea markets, direct mail fundraising, and telephone bank appeals. Chapter Nine discusses these fundraising ideas in detail. Your newsletter plays an important role in publicizing these fundraising events to your supporters.

• *Membership survey.*   It is helpful to include an occasional survey on the back page of your newsletter along with your membership form. The survey will inform you of what human resources you have in the community. It will provide you with new activists. In the survey, ask: Who is interested in serving on the steering committee? Who would like to work on the newsletter? Who is interested in the communications committee? Ask for whatever you need. Also ask for suggestions from your membership. Your members will be impressd that the group's leaders care what they think.

• *Membership list.*   If your organization has no office or post office box, you may want to give your treasurer's name, address, and telephone number on the bottom of the membership form and have all forms mailed to him. The treasurer should save all the forms and compile a list of your new members with their addresses and telephone numbers. This list can be given to all steering committee members, but otherwise your membership list should remain confidential information. You don't want your opposition sending their own mailings to your members.

Your treasurer or someone else on the steering committee should telephone everyone who has kindly volunteered to help in some capacity on the survey response. They should be thanked for volunteering and be invited to the next steering committee meeting with the organization's leaders to learn what their tasks will be.

After your newsletter editor has edited all the articles and put together a draft of the newsletter, at least one other person on your steering committee should proofread the entire newsletter before it goes to the printer. The spelling, grammar, and information should be flawless.

How Should Your Newsletter Look?

The newsletter must look appealing. People will simply not read a sloppy newsletter. But having a professional typeset your entire newsletter is expensive—often too expensive for a budding organization. You want to do as much of the newsletter as possible without having to pay professionals to do the work you can do yourselves. A computer can make this possible. Today, many personal computers can print up a text as professional-looking as an official typesetting job. It is therefore important for your newsletter editor to own or have access to a computer. Or perhaps someone on your steering committee has one.

When you are deciding how your first newsletter should look, it helps enormously to study what other organizations have done. Ask your neighboring housing associations and local environmental organizations for sample copies of their newsletters. Closely examine their appearance and content. Adopt from them what you like and avoid their mistakes. Feel free to ask their newsletter editors for advice. You might also ask the reference librarian at your public library to help you locate information on how to put together a good newsletter, or check with your local community college for seminars on newsletter writing.

Be sure to choose a format that is easy to read. Double-column printing that simulates newspaper columns is very readable and has the extra advantage of fitting more words on every page.

Also make sure to leave room between your articles for clip art, which makes your newsletter visually appealing and therefore more readable. For example, in our local Sierra Club newsletter, we use clip art of trash-covered beaches, leaping deer, soaring eagles, bear cubs, oak leaves, hikers, mountains, forests, and much more. Clip art comes on individual sheets of paper or in booklets of drawings that are camera-ready for your use. All you do is clip a drawing from a sheet or booklet and add it to your newsletter. Clip art is available at art supply stores.

Your newsletter will need a masthead. Have a local typesetter design one for you. This is a one-time expense and well worth it. All your future newsletters, and even your stationery, can carry this design. Alternatively, if someone in your group has artistic ability, then take advantage of that and ask that person to design the masthead. The masthead should be simple in design, representative of your organization, and something that everyone in your group can feel proud of. It should be bold and dignified, not too fancy or complicated.

How to handle headlines? Certain computers have desktop-publishing software programs that print out big, bold headlines. However, if your computer does not, then take the layout of your articles to a local typesetter and have the headlines added to your newsletter. This is generally not too costly and is worth the price. The more readable your newsletter, the more members will sign up and mail in their dues. Newsletters should pay for themselves in the amount of dues they attract.

How to Distribute Your Newsletter

If you have no money for postage, the cheapest way to deliver your first newsletter is the old tried and true hand-delivery method of slipping the newsletter under your neighbors' doormats. Divide up your neighborhood and have every willing member of your steering and communications committees hand-deliver the newsletters to designated streets. Once your membership dues start flowing in, you may never have to do this again. So enjoy the walk.

Eventually you will have enough money for postage. Your treasurer can obtain a bulk mailing permit at the post office to reduce the price of your postage. If your organization has become nonprofit, then you may use the nonprofit mailing rate, which is even cheaper. An indicia of your bulk rate or nonprofit status should be printed onto your newsletter in place of a postage stamp.

You also need mailing labels. Someone in your group may have a computer that can print out address labels. Put this person in charge of your membership mailing list. Every time a new member signs up, that person's name is simply entered into the computer. Then, before each mailing, the computer can print out self-sticking address labels that your communications committee can quickly and easily affix to your newsletters.

If your organization does not have a computer that prints out address labels, then you may have to write out the addresses by hand. At the beginning of my political organizing, I developed countless hand cramps addressing envelopes. The job is lots more fun if your communications committee can meet over snacks and drinks, making a festive occasion of it. It is important to keep morale high, especially when doing drudge work.

If you are fortunate, a cooperative realtor may be on your steering committee. Realtors generally have access through their office computers to the addresses of residents in your area. A realtor in your group could run out labels for you on his office computer, saving a few hand cramps.

Once your organization has collected ample dues, it is time to look for a mailing service. Ask editors of other organizations' newsletters whether they use a mailing service and if they would recommend it.

Mailing services generally have available lists of local residents and their addresses. You may elect to mail to areas in your town by postal route, for example, to make certain that everyone in certain parts of town receives a copy, thereby contacting present allies and potential new members. Or you can simply give the mailing service your own membership list and have them start a file for your organization.

The mailing service takes care of printing the address labels and affixing the labels to your newsletters, then delivering them to the post office for you. You often can use the service's bulk rate permit number. The company can also store your mailing list in its computer files for future mailings. All you have to do is to deliver the folded newsletters to the company from the printer. The mailing service takes care of the rest.

What a great newsletter! You have created a newsletter of which you are proud. It boldly displays a striking masthead, eye-catching clip art, interesting headlines, and fact-filled articles. It looks good, plus it expresses your concerns. So spread it around.

Decision makers will not only read your newsletter, but will also discuss it with their colleagues. Your newsletter alerts the community's power brokers that your environmental concerns are an undeniable fact of life. The power of the written word presents you as a viable force in local issues.

Here is a sample front page of a newsletter:

SIERRA CLUB ⬤ MARIN GROUP

FEBRUARY   NEWSLETTER

TROUBLED WATERS FOR OUR BAY

By Maritza Pick

The Bay Institute has discovered harmful levels of selenium contamination in large state & federal aqueducts which carry water to millions of people in the Bay Area, Southern California and to San Joaquin Valley farms. Selenium is one of the most toxic chemicals to fish & wildlife, reports William T. Davoren, Executive Director of the Bay Institute of San Francisco.

In a letter to Bay Institute members, Davoren states that selenium killed thousands of fish & birds at the Kesterson National Wildlife Refuge, where agricultural waste water was dumped. In the Bay Area, selenium has been found in ducks in the South Bay, San Pablo Bay & Suisun Marsh.

Davoren writes: "To our shock & dismay, an independent scientific testing laboratory showed 12 parts per billion (ppb) of selenium in the state aqueduct & 24 ppb in the federal canal — much more than the level of 2ppb deemed harmful to fish & wildlife. These levels even exceed the safe drinking water standard of 10ppb.

"Selenium is a major killer of fish & wildlife because, like the now-banned pesticide DDT, it 'bio-accumulates,' or builds up, in the tissues of plants & animals. The selenium contamination works its way up the food chain, as fish feed on aquatic organisms, & birds & other wildlife feed on fish. Selenium attacks the reproductive systems of fish & wildlife."

Davoren reminds us that toxics flow into our bay from cities, refineries, farms & factories, loaded with selenium, pesticides & metals. "The Bay Institute has already taken action to limit discharges by oil refineries, resulting in action by the EPA & Bay Area Regional Water Quality Board to establish limits for selenium discharges into the bay, & forcing the oil companies to establish a baywide selenium monitoring program? Davoren urges us now to address selenium from agricultural run-off.

The Bay Institute will conduct a new series of scientific water tests. Plus they will publicize the results & lobby federal & state agencies to stop agricultural waste water dumping into drinking water supplies. They confront the powerful Water Lobby, the coalition of Central Valley & Southern California developers, plus the huge corporate farms, which drain away the life-sustaining fresh water that our bay needs desperately.

Our San Francisco Bay's fresh water supply is dwindling to an appallingly low level. In 1850 the bay received about 27.5 million acre-feet of fresh water. By 1980, only 10.3 million. In the year 2000, it is predicted to be less than 8 million — less than a third of its original flow. We must act now to make sure that our bay survives!

For more information about The Bay Institute of San Francisco, contact them at 10 Liberty Ship Way, Suite 120, Sausalito, CA 94965.

Hear About Greenbelt Treasures

The Sierra Club Marin Group will present a film & discussion about the beauty & protection needed for our Bay Area Greenbelt. Within the nine counties lie nearly 4 million acres of parks, watersheds, farms, ranches, forests & vineyards comprising our Greenbelt. This award-winning film, narrated by Jerry Graham, lets you meet a fascinating set of characters from the unofficial Zen master of vine-pruning to the true blue cowboy working his cattle one hour from downtown San Francisco. From the Mission Blue Butterfly to the antler-crashing Tule Elk of Point Reyes.

This delightful color film & discussion will be presented jointly by the Greenbelt Alliance & the Sierra Club Marin Group. The Greenbelt Alliance promotes open space & is endorsed by over 50 civic & conservation groups representing 100,000 members.

This regular monthly meeting **is open to everyone & is free.** It will be held Wednesday, February 13, 8 p.m., at the Whistlestop Wheels Building in San Rafael, located at 930 Tamalpais Ave. between 3rd & 4th Sts., one block west of Hwy. 101. Parking available in the lots next door.

This newsletter sample demonstrates the appeal of clip art.

♥ BOOK DRIVE ♥
VALENTINES GIFTS

The Sierra Club's Book Drive for Soviet Greens offers you an original and rare idea for a Valentine's Day gift. They are selling beautiful, hand-painted lacquer brooches from Russia. A lovely Valentine's gift for that special someone!

In addition, the Book Drive could use your help in finding storage space, preferably in Marin County. They need a large storage space where they can store, sort, and pack boxes of publications for shipping.

Contact Marcia and Ed Nute in San Rafael.

ENVIRONMENTAL CAREERS

Earth Work is a new monthly magazine offering environmentally oriented careers. A recent issue contained 16 pages of environmental positions worldwide. The magazine also features profiles of people working in various environmental careers. The magazines' publisher is the Student Conservation Association, a non-profit educational organization which provides opportunities for student and adult volunteers.

A one-year subscription costs $29.95. A single issue is $6. For information contact the editorial offices of the Student Conservation Association, 1800 N. Kent St., Suite 913, Arlington, VA 22209. Phone (703) 524-2441.

LEARN
HOW TO SAIL

The California Department of Boating and Waterways announced that boating safety classes will be offered by the U.S. Coast Guard Auxiliary and the U.S. Power Squadrons.

Coast Guard classes will be offered at Fort Bragg on Feb. 26, Petaluma on Feb. 29 and Sausalito on March 3.

Boating safety education courses offered by the Power Squadrons, sail and power boating, will be at Hamilton Air Force Base on Feb. 19. For more info on boating classes, call 1-800-869-7245.

POINT REYES
FIELD SEMINARS

The Point Reyes Field Seminars Program offers spring courses in natural history, photography, environmental education, and the arts, taught by recognized professionals. Class size is limited. Pre-registration is required.

Classes include: Tiptoe through the tidepools, Wildflower hikes, Insects, Butterflies, Moonlight bonfires, Songbirds, Owls, drawing and painting wildflowers, weaving Easter baskets, sketching outdoors, photographing wildlife, and family nature experiences.

For information, call 663-1200.

SLIDE RANCH

Slide Ranch at Muir Beach is a Center for Environmental Education and Agricultural Literacy. Established in 1970 as a non-profit organization, Slide Ranch programs foster a sense of wholeness for children — a personal connection between land, plants, and animals. The goal is for children to grow up to value themselves while protecting the natural environment which sustains all life.

Slide Ranch serves anyone who needs the programs regardless of their ability to pay. It is a rare opportunity for city children to experience the beauty of nature.

One third grader said, "I feel safe here. I finally got it in my head last night that there weren't nobody or no thing gonna hurt me. I like that, feeling safe and all. I want to feel safe when I go back to my neighborhood." She had never been outside at night, because where she lived that would be too dangerous. Fear of the dark was all she knew until she slept at Slide Ranch in a grassy field above the ocean. For the first time she felt safe at night.

If you would like to contribute to Slide Ranch or find out more information about it, call 381-6155.

CHAPTER 4

How to Get Your Issue in
the Newspapers

I t is essential for you to educate the public on the issues. Coverage in your local newspapers is the most efficient way to spread the word about your cause. Moreover, newspapers help create public opinion. Effective use of your local press will be one of your most powerful political tools.

If you are lucky, your local editors will be staunch supporters of your cause. But don't expect the newspapers always to be on your side. The sad truth about local newspapers today is that they are rarely owned locally. A few powerful chains own and run most of the newspapers in the country. As Ben Bagdikian points out in his fine book, *Media Monopoly,* media monopoly is the rule, not the exception. Thus, the owner and publisher of your local newspaper may live on an estate in Connecticut or in a mansion in England. He may not give two figs for your community or its problems. With a few exceptions, long gone is the publisher who lives across town and is just as affected as you by your community's dilemmas.

This indifference often means that newspapers are purely a business proposition. The bigger the profit, the better. Therefore, newspapers generally support population growth in your community. If you are an environmentalist fighting for slow growth, don't expect the newspapers to be on your side. More people means more subscriptions. More businesses in town means more advertisers. Your local newspaper will consider its profit margin first and foremost. Traffic congestion, air pollution, water contamination, and social unrest—these are just stories to cover.

Most newspaper editorial staffs claim neutrality on issues. However, which stories newspapers decide to cover and how they cover them make all the difference to your cause. Newspapers always convey a point of view, merely in the selection of what they choose to focus on and what they decide to ignore.

Do not despair if your local newspapers don't give your organization coverage at first or if the editors are openly hostile to your position. Large newspapers often go through a period of growth vis-à-vis environmental issues. At first, many newspapers resist covering environmental concerns because they view ecology as the enemy of their business interests. In the second stage of growth, newspapers begrudgingly give minor coverage to environmental issues because so many people are writing letters to the editor about them. In the third stage, newspapers realize that your group is growing stronger all the time and creating events and therefore must receive good coverage simply because you truly are making news. Finally, the newspapers will accept you as a force in your community and give you regular coverage whether they agree with you or not.

If your group starts a citywide movement, you may actually cause newspaper editors to understand your point of view and join your cause, if for no other reason than the newspapers will lose readers and advertisers if they consistently ignore the concerns of a majority of their readers.

You must make your issue newsworthy. Fortunately, controversies are newsworthy. As political organizer Saul Alinsky noted in his classic book on organizing, *Rules for Radicals,* every issue can be made controversial. When people begin to vocalize their concerns, the wheels of controversy are set in motion.

First, you must convince your local newspaper editors that

people in your community care about your issue. There is one simple way to do this, even if you are just a handful of concerned citizens. Write letters to the editor.

Letters to the Editor

Writing letters to the editor is the fastest and cheapest way to alert the community about your concerns. The price is right. It's free! Besides, even if a newspaper editor does not agree with your opinion, he will probably publish most of your letters on the editorial page. Many newspapers have a policy of publishing most, if not all, letters to the editor. If your group sends in enough letters, the editor will soon realize that he has a community controversy on his hands. Eventually, the editor will feel compelled to send a reporter to cover your issue.

Letters to the editor accomplish several important goals:

- They inform the general public about your group's concerns.

- They convince the newspaper editor that your issue is worthy of future coverage.

- They garner more support for your cause and more members for your organization.

- They inform local politicians about an issue they will have to deal with whether they like it or not. (Politicians do read these letters.)

- They give your organization and its leadership credibility. Letters to the editor will soon make your organization a household name in your community.

Your letters to the editor will flush out your adversaries. Soon after your letters are published, your opposition will begin mailing in letters to the newspapers to criticize your position. Your natural instinct will be outrage. Don't take the attacks on your position personally. If people are responding to your letters, then they are taking you seriously. Their replies also create more of a controversy. Remember, newspapers thrive on controversy. If a newspaper editor sniffs out major clashes in your community, you can expect even more coverage for your issue.

Don't be afraid of the controversy that develops. You will be shocked to find that all of a sudden you have enemies. People of whom you have never heard will be saying nasty things about your cause and perhaps about you. It's an unpleasant feeling. No one likes to be criticized publicly. However, you can gauge how seriously you are being taken by the intensity of the attacks against you and your organization. If powerful forces in your community are opposing you openly, then congratulations! You have become a force! Opposition is the price you pay for being influential.

How to Organize a Letters-to-the-Editor Campaign

Many people suffer a mental block against putting pen to paper. Even people who are excellent public speakers or superb organizers may loathe writing letters. Many see a blank piece of paper and all their thoughts flee. Therefore you need to find a few people who actually *like* to write letters. These people will be extremely valuable to your organizaiton. They will become your organization's scribes.

Centuries ago, before public education, few people could read or write. In order to compose wills, love letters, or business documents, individuals would visit the local scribe. The scribe would listen carefully to what a person wanted to communicate, then he would write the letter or document. Your organization's scribes will function in much the same way.

You may want to form a letter-writing committee composed of your scribes. However, editors will not continue printing letters with the same few signatures appearing on them. These individuals will soon be taken as crackpots with an ax to grind, and their letters may eventually be ignored by the newspapers. The whole point is to make the press and the public see the letters as part of a large community movement, so you need lots of different signatures on them. Therefore, if people in your organization have good ideas but do not like writing letters, they should be encouraged to telephone your scribes with their ideas and let the scribes type up those ideas in letters for them to sign. You will be pleased how well this system works. Your organization can flood the newspapers with letters to the editor.

As part of your campaign, make a list of all the newspapers in your area, including citywide and countywide papers and papers found in neighboring towns. Don't overlook the small newspapers in your community or any alternative press that may exist. Small, gadfly alternative presses may be the first to take you seriously and do a story on your organization. Then, soon afterward, the larger newspapers will pick up the story. Alternative presses are usually more willing to take risks and investigate a grassroots story, while the larger newspapers remain cautiously distant. But the larger newspapers do not like being scooped by the gadfly papers and usually jump quickly on the bandwagon.

Your area may have a media guide with all the newspapers' addresses, telephone numbers, formats, editors' names, etc. Check with your reference librarian for a media guide to your area.

Once you've made a list of all the newspapers, it's time to write the letters and send copies of them to each appropriate paper. By sending your letters to several newspapers, every letter receives double or triple the exposure.

The copies of your letters should be originals. Newspapers will not print letters that are obvious photocopies. One advantage of using a computer is that it's easy to print out several copies of each letter. If you must use a photocopy machine, then make sure that your copies look just like an original. Some copy machines can do that. But always sign every photocopy with an original signature. It is easy to discern a signature that has been photocopied, and your letters could end up in the editor's trash can.

Tips for Writing Letters to the Editor

• *Learn the appropriate format.* Every newspaper has a specific format for their letters to the editor. Generally, newspapers want letters typed and double-spaced. Often newspapers want you to add your address or telephone number to the letter. Your address and phone number will not be reprinted in the paper. The requirement is merely the editor's way of ascertaining that the letter writer really exists and is a resident of the area.

• *Keep your letters short.* Short letters of a few paragraphs have a better chance of being printed in newspapers. Long letters may not be printed at all because they take up too much room, which could be filled by paying advertisers. Also, even if the editor plans to print one of your long letters, he may wait weeks until he has the extra space for it.

Short letters not only have a better chance of being printed, they have a much better chance of being read. It's a sad truth that people have short attention spans. Consumer advocate Ralph Nader claims that the average American has but a two-minute attention span. So make your letters short and sweet.

If you have a lot to say and simply must say it all, then divide your long letter into two or three short letters. Your relatives or friends can sign the additional letters.

• *Vary the letter styles.* Your letters should reflect all the perspectives possible. Some letters should be sarcastic and others humorous, ironic, statistical, emotional, cool, or rational. Use every angle possible. Present many points of view—those of the businessman, consumer, grocer, homemaker, teacher, parent, environmentalist, etc. Newspaper readers should be able to identify with the various perspectives.

• *Use mockery to assail your opposition.* If your letters ridicule your opposition and make your adversaries' position appear foolish or absurd, so much the better. Always base your statements on documented facts of what your opposition actually stated or did.

• *Don't engage in name-calling or vulgar language.* Newspapers usually won't print letters with vulgar language. No matter how tempting it is to vent your anger by name-calling, never do it in writing. Your letter simply will not be printed.

• *Let the facts speak for themselves.*   It is always best to let the facts incriminate your opposition. It is also effective to use your opposition's own statements against them. Your mayor may have once said, "The citizens of this town are too stupid to realize how beneficial a new pesticide company will be for the local economy. So what if pesticides from the factory leak into the bay from time to time!" Quote statements such as this to your advantage. You discredit both your mayor and the proposed pesticide factory.

How to Deal with Reporters

Once your cause becomes controversial enough, reporters will be telephoning you for statements. A good reporter is looking for notable, quotable statements, so you should keep several things in mind when dealing with them.

• *Measure your words carefully when talking to reporters.* Beware! In their constant search for a good story some reporters will try to incite you to say something that may be misconstrued when taken out of context. Try to make each of your remarks factual, simple, and to the point. Be prepared to have your remarks quoted accurately, but out of the context of your conversation with the reporter. After all, the reporter and her editor have the right to edit the article as they see fit.

For example, during my college days, a friend and I were opposing the massive cutbacks for education in the state university system. A television reporter asked my friend how she was being affected by the cutbacks. My friend replied earnestly to the television camera, "I have been retarded in my graduate studies because the library no longer has funds to purchase important books and journals in my field of research." Later that week, my friend appeared on the local television evening

news saying only, "I have been retarded." A curious bit of editing.

• *When speaking to reporters, remember that you represent your entire organization in the public's eyes.*   Never make personal statements that may offend your organization's members. It requires great self-control, but state your position in a positive way, rather than bashing your opposition with verbal abuse. Reporters and the public will gain respect for your calm diplomacy. Overly emotional, abusive people tend to be viewed as crackpots.

• *Make friends with your local reporters.*   If you see reporters at public meetings, introduce yourself to them. Thank them for their contributions to the community. Very few people ever thank reporters. They will appreciate your kindness and remember you. After a while, your local reporters will know to call you whenever a story affects your neighborhood or your cause. You will gain the advantage of always getting your point of view expressed in their articles.

• *Recommend other people to call.*   If colleagues in your organization are particularly well informed, then recommend to the reporter that she contact these other people, too, for her story. The reporter will be eager to speak to many persons, so be helpful in supplying names and telephone numbers of people who can express your position articulately. The more helpful you are, the better chance you have of seeing your side presented fairly in your local press.

Remember, it's thanks to the newspaper coverage of your letters and activities that your organization will gain credibility in the community. When the press acknowledges your organization, then your entire city becomes aware of your existence. So, no matter what the flaws in your local press, be grateful that it exists. It is your trumpet call to the world.

How to Deal with Editors

When you want to get your issue covered by a newspaper, it is a good tactic for two people from your group to make an appointment with the newspaper's editor. Even if he is openly hostile to your position, it may help for him to hear in person the purpose of your organization and the importance of your cause. You will provide a human face for your issue.

Remember to be polite and friendly with the editor, even if he is initially bosom buddies with your opposition. You want to make it as easy as possible for the editor to change his position to your side eventually. So never antagonize him intentionally. Just present your case calmly and rationally.

Finally, never yell at editors (or reporters). They have memories like elephants and have powerful tools for revenge. I recall one county supervisor who liked to storm into editors' offices to shout at them for the "tripe" they had printed in their newspapers. The editors stoically said nothing. But when the supervisor ran for reelection, the newspapers savaged him and he lost the election.

Freedom of the press is a rare, great gift. Take advantage of this privilege and your organization's cause will gain credibility, renown, and influence. Furthermore, when you are disgusted with the environmental disasters printed in the newspapers, keep in mind: If you don't like the news, go out and make some of your own!

CHAPTER 5

Pitfalls and Rewards of Political Organizing

P olitical activity brings out the best and the worst in people. On the positive side, people often admit that political involvement offers one of the most exciting, fulfilling times of their lives. It is an intense activity that elevates people out of the humdrum routine of work and family. It is a time of devotion to a cause higher than oneself. On the negative side, pitfalls inevitably lie waiting on your path to environmental victory.

Internal Squabbles
Political activists are all too human. They are not saints. They have their share of idiosyncrasies and flaws. Your organization will attract strong personalities who are outspoken and opinionated. Unfortunately, these personalities will inevitably clash. The resulting internal conflicts are by far the most unpleasant aspects of political activity.

It is a shame that allies must battle against one another. But it is a sad fact of life that internal squabbling among allies may defeat you, while your opposition laughs on the sidelines. This internal bickering must be dealt with judiciously and patiently. It must never be allowed to destroy your organization.

Strange Bedfellows

Politics does indeed made strange bedfellows. Your organization may attract Democrats and Republicans, conservatives and radicals, young and old, religious and atheists. The one thing that everyone shares in common is a belief in the cause. They are willing to take time away from their work and play to fight for the success of your issue. Always stress what binds you all together as a group. Avoid discussing unrelated topics on which you all may have different opinions. That's asking for trouble.

Marin County, California, offers an interesting study in strange bedfellows. Environmentalists and ranchers, city and country folk joined forces to preserve an exquisite coast in northern California as Point Reyes National Seashore while dedicating the adjacent grasslands for agriculture. The successful cooperative effort that saved West Marin from massive development has already become a model of survival for rural areas near urban centers.

John Hart's delightful book *Farming on the Edge* relates the history of this unusual alliance. In the book's foreword, Wendell Berry writes, "The people of the urban eastern section wished to keep the rural western section from being covered with subdivisions. They wanted to preserve the 'open space' of West Marin for the sake of all the needs that humans and other creatures have for open space. And they wanted to preserve themselves from the problems of traffic and congestion that would come with massive development 'over the hill.' It became evident that to preserve the open space they needed the farmers. And it became equally evident to the farmers that, to survive, they needed the sympathy, support, and help of the city people; they saw that, by themselves, they did not have the power to determine their own future."

After a rocky start, these unusual allies came to the agreement that the ranchers give up the idea of selling their land for development, and in turn the urban population would help agriculture flourish. It is important to understand that Point Reyes National Seashore was seen as a great victory by environmen-

talists, but the ranchers viewed the park as the beginning of the end of agriculture in the region. However, the new bond between the two traditionally opposing forces proved that cooperation was the best way to satisfy the rural and urban residents. Marin County had once been California's major dairy land. Thanks to the recent joint efforts toward farmland protection, it remains beautiful farmland.

One of the positive aspects of environmental crises is precisely this cooperation among people for the common good. Warren County, North Carolina, provides another example of newfound allies working successfully together for environmental victory.

In 1978, the governor of North Carolina declared the state's intention to dispose of PCB-tainted soil at a new dump site in Warren County. The citizens of Warren County were shocked. They wondered how the state would even dare consider doing this when the water table at the proposed location was within fifteen feet of the bottom of the dump, much less than the fifty feet the Environmental Protection Agency (EPA) generally suggested between water and waste.

The organization Warren County Citizens Concerned About PCBs was formed and declared that their county had been designated because it had little political influence. Its population was 64 percent Native American and black. The county's average income was the lowest in the state. Some people in Warren County perceived the decision as racist.

For nearly three years, the residents fought the proposed dump with legal action—in vain. In 1982, the state and the EPA agreed to build the dump.

Outraged, more than a hundred demonstrators blocked the landfill entrance to prevent the first delivery of toxic soil. Fifty-five marchers were arrested. The governor refused to meet with the protesters.

Undeterred, demonstrators continued blocking the trucks for two weeks. Eventually 520 persons were arrested. Community meetings drew more than a thousand individuals. Students from the University of North Carolina at Chapel Hill came to Warren County to join the demonstrations.

For Warren County, this brought blacks and whites together, forging new bonds and breaking from the grim tradition of segregated political agendas. Close friendships were formed in the joint struggle.

Finally, national publicity pressured the governor to meet with the protest leaders. The governor vowed to keep future landfills out of Warren County, thereby easing one of the greatest fears of the residents that this landfill would only be the beginning of many to come, making Warren County the state's dumping ground.

The landfill for the PCB-tainted soil was built. However, Warren County residents have successfully worked together to keep other landfills out of their county, including blocking a

1990s new proposal to locate an enormous, regional, five-county landfill there. Public pressure simply would not allow it. In union there is strength.

Contradictions and Compromise

You may find yourself endorsing a political candidate who supports your cause even though you disagree with her on every other issue. You may find yourself with colleagues who are irascible people but who are useful to your goals because they are effective organizers. In organizing, you must be prepared to deal with unexpected people and issues. Remain flexible and tolerant. To make the best of it, accentuate whatever is useful and constructive in a person or a situation, and downplay the irritating aspects. Above all, remember: never burn your bridges. In other words, never make an enemy unnecessarily. You never know when you may need that person in the future.

Troublemakers

One diplomatic chore of your organization's leadership is to distance disruptive volunteers from your steering committee. Some people will come to your meetings only to shoot off their mouths. They are full of vague notions, heated emotions, and malicious gossip. Often these same people are not willing to do one lick of practical work. Meanwhile all their useless chatter has taken time away from essential matters.

Do not invite these people back to your steering committee meetings. There is no need to alienate them or insult them. Just don't invite them back. They may prove useful at city council meetings when you need a large, vocal attendance.

For example, one urban environmental group found themselves on the same side of an issue as a clique of crusty old horsemen living on the rural outskirts of the city. There would be no way that the city environmentalists and the hard-drinking cantankerous horse lovers could ever agree on anything except their mutual desire to save the local river from pollution from a factory upstream.

The horsemen hated steering committee meetings and disrupted them with their rowdy humor. To everyone's relief, the city environmentalists told the horsemen that they need not attend any more steering committee meetings. The independent-minded horsemen were thrilled with their regained freedom. But at the environmentalists' request, they gladly did show up at all the public hearings in a large, impressive group. Their attire of cowboy hats and boots made for a dramatic entrance at city-hall public hearings. These free-spirited men were part of the folklore and history of the town, and their presence made an important statement to the city council.

Fragile Egos

People whose egos outweigh the cause have no place on your steering committee. If someone does not believe that the success of your cause is more important than his ego, then drop him like a hot potato. He is trouble for certain. A cooperative group spirit is vital for every steering committee member. Teamwork will lead to success; squabbling will lead to defeat. Abraham Lincoln's quote that "A house divided against itself cannot stand" is especially true for any budding organization.

On the other hand, a good community organizer knows how important it is to stroke egos, to pat people on the back, and thank people publicly. Always applaud people's good ideas. You may even want to give other people credit for your own ideas. A good organizer is lavish with praise and generous with compliments.

Politicians' Thin Skin

You would expect politicians to have the hides of rhinoceroses after all the public and private abuse that they endure. But surprisingly, many politicians are thin-skinned. Their egos bruise easily. Any politician has some percentage of his constitutents liking him and some percentage hating him over any given issue. People are always yelling at him. Like any other human being, a politician prefers to be liked.

I have seen amazing success stories of grassroots environmental leaders who are able to seduce opposing politicians over to their side. This is accomplished by treating any politician as a potential friend. Take him out to lunch. Meet for coffee. Compliment him on some of his better policies. Ask him for advice. Ask him about his background, his family, his hobbies. What do you have in common with him?

Simply by treating a politician with friendly respect and appreciation, you may win him over to your side. He may open his mind just enough to value your point of view. You won't change his philosophy of life or politics, but you may be able to sway his vote to your side on a certain issue. That could mean victory for your cause.

For example, one housing association in a city in Washington was fighting to preserve a nearby forest from a lumber company's chainsaw. The city council majority openly endorsed the lumber company's plans to cut down the forest to make more room for commercial and residential development in order to expand the city and bring in a larger tax base. The housing association realized that it had to change the opinion of just one member of the city council in order to swing the upcoming city council vote in its favor. The association's steering committee decided that the mayor might be the one most likely to sit down and listen to their side, even though she had already publicly endorsed the lumber company's plans.

The steering committee met several times with the mayor. By chatting amiably with her, they found out that the mayor harbored fond memories of her childhood in a town nestled in the lush forests of Washington. The steering committee played up the mayor's nostalgia for her rustic youth until she finally understood the value of preserving this particular forest. Later, at the city council hearing, the mayor shocked every developer in town by voting to preserve the forest.

Mixed Loyalties

Someone with mixed loyalties can be dangerous to your organization. This person is a potential traitor to your cause. Unfortunately, it is not always possible to sniff out someone's mixed loyalties until it is too late. A certain amount of secrecy is necessary to your organization's success. You don't want your opposition to find out about your strategies. You ought to feel free to speak openly among your steering committee. If you suspect that someone may have strong sympathies toward your opposition, then try to ease that person out of your steering committee. This person may be an intentional or unwitting spy for your opposition. Beware.

Gossip

Deal with facts, not gossip. Most of what you learn about local government will be taught to you by word of mouth. Take all you hear with a grain of salt. Try to determine what is fact and what is mere gossip.

There is far too much gossip and speculation in political circles. This gossip often passes for fact and takes on a life of its own. At the beginning, you will spend a good deal of time trying to separate truth from speculation. Some well-meaning people will supply you with so-called information that is pure fiction. Soon you will notice who supplies fact and who provides fiction. People tend to be consistent about this. Be careful that you and your steering committee deal only with facts. You will lose credibility quickly if you do not have your facts straight at all times.

I have known many victims of untrue rumors. For example, it was well known in one Massachusetts town that a friend of mine had been an active political campaigner for years. However, he decided to take a one-year sabbatical from local politics. But no one believed that he could sit idly on the sidelines in that year's city council election, and during the election he received nasty calls from both sides. Each side assumed that he was the brains behind the campaign for the other side. It would have been very simple for the rumormongers to verify that he wasn't taking part in the campaigns in any way. But the rumors continued to spread. He was blamed for outlandish campaign practices that he would never have endorsed, even if he had been active in the election. Eventually he learned that all he could do was laugh about the ridiculous rumor mill.

Here's another example. An environmental group was opposing the widening of a road that would have turned a quiet street into a highway of traffic. The chairman of the planning commission swore that the widening of this road had been approved years ago. All the politicians were acting on the basis that such approval had already been secured. It took one lone resident of that street to check back to the documents on file at city hall to discover that, in fact, widening of the street had never been approved. The policy makers were forming decisions based on pure rumor, not fact.

The message is clear. Always verify your facts. Go to the source. Moreover, seek out original documents whenever possible.

Anger

Most members of your organization will feel anger about the issues you are addressing. How dare the oil companies think of drilling off the coast near pristine beaches? How dare the government consider putting a toxic waste dump only a few miles from your home? How dare the lumber companies use herbicides that poison the groundwater of your town? How dare a condominium complex pave over valuable farmland near your ranch? How dare the factory in your city continue to spill dangerous waste into the river? There may be countless reasons why you are organizing and why you feel anger.

It is essential to control your anger and funnel it into constructive action. "Don't get angry, get even!" is a good motto to live by. Even better, remember the saying: "When tempers reach a boiling point, ideas evaporate. Keep a cool head!"

When people get angry, they say things they later regret. They can also reveal too much or give the wrong impression. It is vitally important for your organization first to arouse the outrage of the community and then to channel this outrage into effective action. Pure rage is a wasted emotion.

Your newsletters and informative meetings give your community a chance to ask questions, to be educated on the issues. An informed community is an activist community. There are three steps you can use to channel anger into useful activism: (1) arouse your community's outrage through informative newsletters and letters to the editor of local newspapers; (2) organize community meetings where people can ask questions and express their concerns; and (3) create committees so that people can volunteer to put their outrage and knowledge to work.

In her foreword to Nicholas Freudenberg's book *Not in Our Backyards!* Lois Marie Gibbs tells how anger galvanized her to action: "In 1978 I was a Niagara Falls housewife living in a neighborhood called Love Canal. I found chemicals in my own backyard and these chemicals were hurting my children. I tried it the nice way. . . . Then I got angry. And then I fought by organizing my neighbors into the United States' first citizens' organization fighting hazardous waste. We won. . . . So can you. And so can we all."

The story of Love Canal is a tale of a community organizing from fear and anger.

Love Canal's history is terrifying. William Love, a nineteenth-century entrepreneur, planned to build a model city around a canal between the upper and lower portions of the Niagara River. However, due to lack of funds, the project was halted. The partially completed canal became a place for swimming and ice skating.

Then, in 1947, Hooker Chemical began dumping there. It is estimated that between 1947 and 1952, more than 43 million pounds of chemical wastes were dumped into Love Canal by Hooker. Three ounces of dioxin, one of the most poisonous substances on earth, can kill more than a million people. Nevertheless, 130 pounds of dioxin were dumped into Love Canal.

The chemicals were buried. Eventually, grass and weeds grew over them, creating a field that children used as a playground. Since 1953 the board of education owned the property. They had needed the land, and Hooker sold it to them for one dollar, signing a contract that absolved Hooker of any problems resulting from the field.

Between the 1950s and mid-1970s, many Love Canal residents poked fun at anyone who complained of the poor air, land, or water quality. Nonetheless, poisonous clouds floated over the homes, black ooze seeped into basements, craters formed in the baseball fields, housepaint turned black, and children were burned playing on the field as chemicals popped up through the soil.

City and state officials simply did not want to acknowledge the problem. After all, Hooker was a major employer in the region. Yet babies were born with cleft palates, double rows of bottom teeth, three ears, and disintegrating eardrums. Fifty-six percent of the babies born from 1974 to 1978 had birth defects. Mothers were horrified, and homemakers organized. Only when the situation drew international news coverage did authorities feel compelled to take some action. Lois Marie Gibbs and Love Canal's homemakers attracted this attention through their grassroots community organization.

Finally, President Carter declared Love Canal a disaster area and designated the first funds provided for the clean-up of a human-made disaster. Meanwhile, the residents still lived at the site and were exposed to the poisons daily. In 1979, only one child was born healthy from the fifteen pregnancies in Love Canal.

Eventually, President Carter declared a second federal emergency and allowed families to be relocated with federal funds.

Lois Marie Gibbs, founder of the Love Canal Homeowners Association, organized a small, blue-collar community and successfully took on city hall, the state, and the White House. Gibbs continues the battle. She is director of the Citizens' Clearinghouse for Hazardous Wastes, an organization that advises grassroots environmental groups nationwide on how to deal with local hazardous-waste issues.

Indifference

Initially, most people in your community may feel indifferent toward your cause. People get involved to the degree that they feel personally threatened or rewarded by a situation. It is your organization's jodb to awaken the community from its indifferent slumber.

Indifference originates from two main sources. The first source of indifference is ignorance. People are not informed, and therefore they don't care out of ignorance of the facts. It is the task of your organization to inform the public through rousing newsletters and informative letters to the editor. Your role is that of community educator. You are the teacher; community members are your students; the city is the classroom.

People are worried about their kids' grades, car repairs, crises at work, mortgage payments, a mother-in-law's upcoming visit, marital woes, etc. Deluged with personal problems, people tend to hope that some mysterious "they" will take care of the community's problems. You must convince people that there is no "they." We are "they." Help people understand that if they are not part of the solution, then they are part of the problem.

The second main source of indifference is despair, which leads to complacency. Many people feel that our environmental problems are overwhelming and that the individual cannot do anything to change the situation. You must convince your neighbors that indeed everyone can make a difference. The emergence of your grassroots organization in itself will inspire many people and give them hope. As the British philosopher Edmund Burke said, "Nobody makes a greater mistake than he who did nothing because he could only do a little."

Every little bit counts. Some people are able to give money but have no free time for meetings. Others are able to write letters but have no money to donate. Some can be active on telephone committees but are too shy to speak at public hearings. Then there are the many who will turn up at your important public meetings with officials and politicians. Though they may sit silently, they are there in large numbers, and their mere presence speaks loudly to your community's leaders.

You should make everyone feel useful. Everyone has a special ability that can benefit your community. Allow people a chance to express their outrage in whatever way their abilities permit. It is an important task of your organization's leadership to tap the tremendous reserves of talent in your community.

The key to dealing with people is to bring out the best in everyone for the success of your organization's efforts. As Andre Bacard advises in his book *Hunger for Power: Who Rules the World and How,* follow the Golden Rule of Organizing: "Af-

firm the best in others as you would have others affirm the best
in you."

Environmental Heroes as Inspiration

When environmental battles get tough, it helps to keep in mind
inspiring leaders such as John Muir, a lone wolf who felt more
comfortable on solitary hikes in the wilderness than at public
hearings. Yet John Muir led the way to the creation of Yosemite
National Park and the Sierra Club. As anthropologist Margaret
Mead asserted, a handful of people can change the world.
Never lose heart. If you acquaint yourself with local and international environmental heroes, their example will inspire you
and keep you going strong.

The 1992 Goldman Environmental Prize winners provide
inspiration to activists around the world. Following are brief
biographical sketches of these dedicated activists.

Colleen McCrory of Canada has crusaded for nearly twenty
years to protect the world's largest temperate rainforest in British Columbia, plus the endangered boreal forests stretching
across northern Canada.

McCrory grew up with her eight brothers and sisters in the
Valhalla Mountains of British Columbia. A high school drop-
out and a single mother of three, she operated a small general
store. Colleen became involved in conservation when she realized that logging and mining development threatened the
mountains where she lived. In 1971, she established the Valhalla Wilderness Society. After eight years of intensive lobbying and campaigning, the 49,600-hectare Valhalla Provincial
Park was established in 1983.

Although exhausted after this successful campaign, she
pursued her fight to protect the endangered forests of the
Queen Charlotte Islands in British Columbia. McCrory cofounded the National Save South Moresby Committee. The local pro-logging newspaper, *Red Neck News,* led a smear
campaign against McCrory and other South Moresby supporters. Her life was threatened and her store was boycotted. Even-

tually she was forced to sell it. However, she never gave up her dream, and in 1987 the South Moresby National Park Reserve in the Queen Charlotte Islands was established.

After these two stunning victories, McCrory became the coordinator of the British Columbia Environmental Network, as well as a legislative assistant to a member of Canada's Parliament. She created Canada's Future Forest Alliance, an umbrella organization representing 1 million Canadians concerned about the future of Canada's boreal forests. The alliance spans a broad cross section of groups, including native communities and labor unions. McCrory continues to work for her goal of preserving 12 percent of Canada's land base as wilderness.

Medha Patkar of India has been the central organizer of a grassroots movement to stop the construction of a series of dams on India's largest westward-flowing river, the Narmada.

The Narmada Valley Development Project is the world's biggest river development scheme, proposing to construct 30 major dams, 135 medium-size dams, and 3000 small dams on the Narmada River and its tributaries. Upon completion, just the Sardar Sarovar Dam alone would submerge more than 12,000 hectares of fertile agricultural land and 13,744 hectares of forest land. It would displace almost 100,000 villagers, mostly from tribal communities.

In 1984, Patkar, a social worker, began working with the tribes in the 248 affected villages, explaining their rights to them. But when she observed that no adequate resettlement plan existed, she plunged headlong into opposition of all the dams proposed for the Narmada Valley. As a result of strong opposition, the World Bank dropped its plans to fund a second large dam, the Narmada Sagar.

Her efforts also led the Japanese government to withdraw its funding of Narmada Sagar, and members of the European Parliament have asked the World Bank to cease financing the project.

Traveling on foot with a small backpack, dressed in sandals and a sari, in Gandhian tradition, she spends lonely weeks

in remote villages, listening to people's problems. She has mo-
bilized thousands of men and women in rallies and marches
against the project. For many, this was the first time that they
had ever protested in such a way.

In the summer of 1991, tribal people from the village of
Manibelli pledged that they would drown rather than move as
authorities threatened to evict the villagers prior to flooding by
monsoons. The protesters were arrested and Patkar went into
hiding.

Patkar devotes her life to protecting the Narmada River and
its people. This dedication increasingly puts her at risk. She
has been beaten and arrested by the police, although the sit-
ins she organizes are peaceful. She even came close to death
after a twenty-two-day hunger strike. Her struggle to save the
river continues.

Christine Jean of France has been a central figure in the
grassroots movement to oppose the plans to dam the Loire—
France's longest, wildest, and most famous river. For more
than three years, Christine Jean has traveled thousands of
miles up and down the length of the Loire as part of her campaign to save it from being dammed.

In the early 1980s, a group of regional authorities, the Public Agency for the Management of the River Loire, made plans
to domesticate the Loire by building dams on the upper part of
the river and its major tributaries.

Christine Jean began by organizing the small, local opposition groups along the river into one strong national organization, S.O.S. Loire Vivante (Living Loire Committee). This
national coalition of environmental groups gained the support
of the World Wildlife Fund.

Her dynamic leadership provided Loire Vivante with unified, constructive opposition to the dam project. As an agron-
omist with a master's degree in ecology, her scientific
expertise helped her successfully lobby pro-dam officials,
counter water engineers' arguments, and inform the French
public about an issue that touched a nerve in French national
pride.

The French dubbed her "Madame Loire" as she gathered support from around the country. Meanwhile, protesters camped at the site of the planned Serre de La Fare dam, outside the Auvergne town of Le Puy. Twice during the two-year encampment protesters prevented bulldozers from beginning construction.

The campaign has become the most popular environmental issue in France in the last twenty years. "Europe's last wild river" has gained widespread European support. Ten thousand supporters from all over Europe showed up at an anti-dam demonstration in Le Puy in 1989.

Finally, in July of 1991, the central government caved in to public pressure and canceled plans to build the Serre de La Fare dam and a second controversial dam at Chambonchard. The long, upper part of the Loire will not be dammed—a tremendous victory!

The battle continues, however. Plans to construct other dams on the Cher and Allier tributaries of the Loire remain under consideration.

Carlos Alberto Ricardo of Brazil is a founder of one of his country's most important social, environmental, and human rights organizations, the Center for Ecumenical Documentation and Information (CEDI).

When newly democratic Brazil was creating its constitution in 1988, powerful agricultural and mining interests were lobbying to reduce the already limited rights of indigenous peoples. Ricardo prepared a report entitled "Mining Companies and Indigenous People in the Amazon." The report revealed to the public which groups had an interest in denying land rights and opening up mining operations in the Amazon. National concern was awakened, resulting in stronger constitutional guarantees for Brazil's indigenous tribes.

In the 1970s, Ricardo cofounded the Committee for the Creation of the Yanomami Park (CCPY), a Brazilian nonprofit organization devoted to protection of the Yanomami, the Amazon's largest indigenous group of people. Eight thousand Yanomami live in the rainforest near Brazil's border with

Venezuela. Yanomami lands were invaded by more than 45,000 gold miners and squatters, who disrupted traditional ways of life and introduced infectious diseases that killed 1000 Yanomami in just three years.

In 1991, the long, difficult struggle to protect Yanomami lands resulted in a great success when Brazil's President Collor issued a decree creating a continuous reserve of 94,000 square kilometers for the Yanomami people.

Wadja Mathieu Egnankou is a young scientist from the Ivory Coast who has been a lone voice for the protection of West Africa's remaining coastal mangrove forests. Traveling from village to village, Egnankou works with coastal communities, teaching them how to care for their diminishing resource. As a nursery for many types of fish, mangroves play a crucial role in the food chain. Mangroves also stop erosion, one of West Africa's most severe problems.

Egnankou has influenced international institutions working in the area by illustrating that environmental concerns impact economics as well as endangered species. In 1989, the African Development Bank decided to finance a road traversing the country's last largely intact mangroves and rainforests. Egnankou succeeded in convincing the engineers that, in reality, it would be less expensive to reroute the road out of the most sensitive areas.

The finest specialist in coastal problems in West Africa, Dr. Egnankou perseveres in his mission to educate local communities, international lending institutions, and governments about the value of the vanishing mangrove.

Jeton Anjain, a senator in the Marshall Islands Parliament, led the evacuation of his community from the Rongelap Atoll, contaminated by United States nuclear testing.

The Goldman Environmental Foundation offered a vivid description of the events in its announcement of the award to Jeton Anjain: "In 1954, the United States exploded the 'Bravo' hydrogen bomb on the Bikini Atoll in the Pacific. It was the largest nuclear weapons device ever detonated by the United

States, 1,300 times the destructive force of the bomb dropped on Hiroshima. That morning the wind was blowing towards the Rongelap Atoll, 100 miles away, where 82 islanders were exposed to extremely high levels of radioactive fallout. The white-powdered fallout covered the islands and, thinking that it was snow, the children played in it. By night, the islanders had become acutely ill. It was not until two days later that the United States evacuated everyone to another island. Then, in 1957, even though the soil, water, and food remained contaminated, these people were returned to Rongelap, along with an additional 200 islanders who were not on Rongelap during the test. United States officials assured the islanders that no radiation danger remained. However, serious medical problems soon developed, including thyroid cancer, leukemia, and the birth of unformed fetuses."

In 1982, the Department of Energy released a study on the islands. Jeton Anjain, trained as a dentist, was then serving as health minister. He questioned the results of the study. Resigning his ministerial post, he felt that he could better represent the people of Rongelap as a senator to the Marshall Islands Parliament. However, the Marshall Islands and American governments refused him assistance in evacuating Rongelap. At long last, in 1985, Anjain succeeded in organizing the evacuation of Rongelap with the help of the *Rainbow Warrior,* the Greenpeace ship.

In 1991, Anjain finally obtained U.S. congressional support as the House and Senate appropriated $3 million to fund an independent health and radiological study on the atoll, the first study of its kind in the world. A clean-up and humanitarian assistance fund was also established.

Whenever your environmental activism leads you onto rocky, difficult paths, recall these heroes. Their strength, dedication, and courage will inspire you to overcome any pitfall.

CHAPTER 6

🌲

The Public Hearing Process

T he fate of many local environmental issues is often sealed
at public hearings. The quality and quantity of the presentations made by your supporters at these public hearings can
determine the victory or defeat of your environmental goals.
Your organization's hard work has been leading to this crucial
event, this day of judgment: the public hearing.

All your organizing so far is really a dress rehearsal for public hearings. A hearing is living theater with your community as
the actors. It has all the elements of good drama: heroes, vil-
lains, noble causes, and always a touch of comedy. Your allies
at public hearings will be experiencing stage fright before their
speeches. There is an air of tension and excitement in the
meeting hall.

The commissioners and officials perch upon their raised
dais like a row of King Solomons. Your supporters squirm in
their chairs in the audience, nervous about the short speeches
that they have prepared to give and hopeful for a favorable outcome. Everyone is wondering: Will our presentations go well?
Do we have more speakers than the opposition? Will our side
prevail? Will the commissioners comprehend the wisdom of
our environmental cause and vote in our behalf?

At a typical public hearing, the mayor or chairman opens

the meeting with a few words, briefly describing the issues to be decided on; then the commission's staff members explain succinctly the project in question. The commissioners ask for clarifications from the staff members. Then the main proponents of the project are allowed to make a presentation. Afterward, members of the public are permitted one by one to approach the podium's microphone and state their endorsements or objections to the project.

After the public testimony is concluded, the commissioners ask more questions of the staff, the project's proponents, and sometimes even the public. Finally, each commissioner proclaims his or her view about the project. When discussion is exhausted, one of the commissioners makes a motion to approve the project, to reject it, to return it to staff for further study, or to send the project's proponents back to the drawing board to alter and improve their plans. The entire commission then votes on the motion.

If your side has prepared well for a public hearing, it can be a thrilling and satisfying experience. You can sway the decision makers to vote for your cause.

There are a variety of public hearings that you may need to attend. Even the smallest of projects—let's say, the creation of a corner city park—may require review and approval by the parks and recreation commission, the city planning commission, the design review commission, and the city council. Other types of projects may involve the board of supervisors, public works commission, coastal commission, etc. The type and number of hearings depend on what kind of issue you are dealing with and whether your issue is within city, county, state, or federal jurisdiction. For example, if you are working to protect five hundred acres of wetlands from being filled, then you may have to prepare for numerous public hearings, including all of the above, plus hearings with local, state, and federal agencies dealing with wetlands protection, water quality control, fish and wildlife, parks and open space, and so on. Every public hearing reviews pertinent facets of a project, encouraging thorough investigation and analysis of its pros, cons, and alternatives.

If you are lucky, your particular issue may require you to prepare for only one important public hearing. That single hearing may decide the fate of your project. However, usually more than one public hearing is necessary to win your fight.

It is tempting to grumble and groan about all the public hearings that your group must attend. But remain grateful for this democratic procedure. The hearing process is designed to permit the public maximum input during the environmental review process. It offers opportunities for grassroots organizations to take a public stand and present a convincing case to decision makers. It is quite likely that a public hearing or a series of them will decide the outcome of your environmental battle.

Of course, when the public hearing process disappoints you and endorses your opposition, you have recourse to a variety of alternatives: petitions, lawsuits, demonstrations, referendums, initiatives, recalls, legislative lobbying, and the election of new public officials. However, if your organization learns to use the public hearing process successfully, and if your community has elected responsive public officials, then the other alternatives may never be necessary.

Your elected officials are extremely important during the public hearing process. For example, the hearings before elected officials such as the city council or board of supervisors may lead to the definitive vote on your environmental issues. Moreover, these elected officials appoint commissioners to such bodies as the public works commission, parks and recreation commission, planning commission, and so on. Obviously, the elected officials tend to appoint commissioners with similar philosophies to their own. An environmentally concerned city council is likely to appoint environmentally astute commissioners. Part II of this guidebook will help you with the important task of electing environmentalists to public office.

If your elected officials, such as city council members, vote in your behalf, then their positive endorsement of your environmental goals will carry much weight if and when your issue must be voted on by other commissions. Other local public hearings may involve such boards as the sanitation district, fire district, water district, housing board, community service district, and city/county boundary commissions.

Although many public hearings may await your organization, none is more important than your first. That first hearing will teach you how to prepare for every public hearing to come. Furthermore, if your organization can produce an impressive showing at your first public hearing, it will gain tremendous credibility and influence overnight.

For example, one fledgling environmental grassroots organization was created to save four hundred acres of prime grazing land from a gigantic residential and commercial urban-development proposal. All the politicians and bureaucrats at city hall endorsed the development. The developer was a friend of everyone in local power. He claimed that the development included "affordable housing," which then gave the project a political halo, no matter how environmentally unsound it was. It looked like the new environmental group didn't stand a chance of winning. No one took the group seriously.

But the members organized furiously. At the first planning commission hearing on the project, the group had two hundred people in attendance, overflowing city hall. Never had so many people showed up for any controversy in that town. It became an historic event. The group had forty prepared and rehearsed speakers ready to present succinct, factual statements in favor of preserving the grazing land. The turnout was so impressive that the development project died that night. The astonished developer withdrew his plans and sold the land.

Overnight, the little environmental group became one of the most powerful and respected conservation forces in the county. This story is not unusual. Grassroots victories usually are tales of Davids winning over Goliaths.

Public Hearings for Environmental Reviews

Many states, counties, and cities require by law that projects go through a public environmental review, although specific regulations vary from state to state. The following comments apply specifically to preparation for a public hearing for review of an Environmental Impact Report (EIR). However, apply the following recommendations to your own public hearings agenda. What succeeds for EIR hearings works for all kinds of public hearings.

What Is an Environmental Impact Report?
An EIR is a document assembled by a consulting firm of various land-use analysts who evaluate the environmental impacts of a project. Depending on the scope of the development being analyzed, this document can be short or contain as

many as several hundred pages. You may pick up copies of an EIR at your local planning department, which may charge a few dollars for each copy.

What does an EIR cover? The EIR assesses how the project will affect all aspects of your environment. The following list provides only a small sampling of all the environmental issues that must be thoroughly studied in a good EIR.

- How will the project affect the community's traffic?

- Will the project add air and noise pollution?

- Will the project be detrimental to wetlands or ridgelines?

- How many trees will be cut down to build the project?

- Is landfill necessary? Where will the landfill come from?

- Will construction of the project destroy anything valuable on the site, such as an Indian burial ground or archeological site?

- Is the project to be built on or near an earthquake fault?

- Is there periodic flooding on the site?

- Is the land at present a valuable agricultural resource?

- Are there any toxics in the soil? Will the project add any toxics?

- How will existing wildlife be affected by the project?

- Are there any endangered species on the site?

Scoping Session
At the initial stages of preparing an EIR, your planning department should hold a public scoping session. At this scoping session before the planning commission, your organization has a chance to list all the issues that you feel deserve attention in the EIR. Bring up every little detail possible. You may present your comments as a series of questions, as illustrated above.

Present your concerns in writing as well as orally at this scoping session. By law, whatever issue you mention at this scoping session must be dealt with in the EIR. Give the EIR consultants lots to think about and plenty to do!

After this scoping session, depending on the scale of the project, the consulting firm often takes six months, a year, or even longer to complete the preliminary EIR. This will give you a breathing spell to strengthen your organization and to sway public opinion in your favor.

The EIR Public Review Hearing

When the initial draft of the EIR is completed, the planning department mails notices to the presidents of all concerned organizations on its mailing list. Make certain that your organization's president and mailing address are listed with the planning department. The notice will indicate the place, date, and time of the upcoming EIR public review hearing. The notice will also explain how and where to obtain copies of the EIR. The responsibility then falls on the shoulders of your organization's steering committee to notify your members about the public hearing through your newsletter.

If it is to your organization's advantage to delay a project, then the EIR process is your opportunity to delay a project for years. Every time an EIR is found inadequate by the planning commission, the entire document must go back to the consultants for revision. It may take the consultants another six months to a year to revise the EIR. Therefore, your job is to identify as many inadequacies in the EIR as is humanly possible.

Why are delays useful? They can be helpful for several reasons. For one, delaying the project gives your organization more time to gather support from the community. Also, long delays may drive the project's financial backers to abandon their proposal. Finally, you may need a delay to change the political slant of your city council. If you know that a majority of your city council endorses the project, then you need to get involved in the next city council election to make certain that environmentally aware candidates run for office and are elected. If the next election is some time away, delays at the environmental review level are useful.

The EIR makes for lengthy and tedious reading. It is unfair to impose the entire document on one person in your organization. It is a lot of work. Also, no matter how capable that one person is, he is bound to miss a few key points that other members in your organization could detect.

Therefore, divide the EIR into sections. Assign each section to one or more volunteers for their commentary. Remember, all you have to do is raise questions as to what information is missing or inaccurate in the EIR.

Try to divide the report so that volunteers have an intrinsic interest in their sections. If you have a chemist in your organization, let her deal with the soil analysis. If you have a construction worker, let him deal with construction issues. If you have someone who lives next to a noisy street, let him analyze the section on traffic. If you have a homemaker with seven kids, let her deal with the section on parks and safety for children. If a member suffers from asthma, urge him to examine the air pollution statistics. You will be astonished at the resources and expertise that the members of your organization can offer.

Make sure you get other environmental groups involved in the EIR process too. Be certain that every possible environmental or other organization in your area writes up and presents a critique of the EIR at the public hearings: local chapters of the Sierra Club, the Audubon Society, other conservation leagues, housing associations, agricultural groups, ranchers, civic groups, school boards, even the fire and police departments if they are sympathetic to your cause. Appeal to every conceivable organization in your community for their involvement. At the EIR hearings, you need to attack the project from as many angles as possible.

Finally, keep in mind that you can use the environmental review process to stop small projects as well as large ones. For example, a powerful corporation bought up parcels of vacant land in one quiet residential neighborhood. Soon the shocked neighbors read in their local newspaper that the corporation planned to build an enormous chemical research center on the vacant meadowland. The city council voted in favor of the corporation against the vocal protests of the neighborhood.

The city council also deemed that no EIR was necessary for approval of the research center.

The neighborhood was angry. They formed a neighborhood association, collected dues, hired an attorney, and went to court. The judge agreed with the neighborhood. He ordered that an environmental review was required before the city council could approve the research center.

This judicial process took a year. Then the EIR on the chemical research center took another year to prepare. Therefore, the neighborhood association gained the time to become actively involved in city council elections to make certain that new city council members were elected who favored the concerns of the neighborhood over big business.

How to Prepare for Public Hearings

Maximizing Attendance

You must spare no effort to assure maximum attendance at a public hearing. Your communications committee should mail out notices to your members about the meeting, stating when, where, and why the hearing is being held. The notice can be in the form of a newsletter, a short note, or a postcard. It depends on how much information your membership needs before the public hearing. If your members need to be updated on the latest details of the project, then mail them an information-packed newsletter. If your community is already well informed on the issue, then postcard notification may be adequate. Following is an example of a short note advising people of a public hearing.

Dear Neighbor:

Your involvement is essential to stop the toxic dumping occurring along our local coastline. Please attend the next city council meeting to tell our public officials why we demand clean, safe beaches.

Meeting: City council public hearing about toxic dumping along our coastline
When: May 2, 8:00 P.M.
Where: City Hall, 12 Government Street

For more information about the event, call Sandy Seal, president of the Save Our Coast Coalition, at 111-2222.

Only if our community cares enough to speak out can we stop the poisoning of our coastline. BE THERE. ONLY YOUR PARTICIPATION CAN SAVE OUR BEACHES!

Cordially,

Your neighbors in the Save Our Coast Coalition

In these notices, certain words should be used as often as possible, such as "you," "your," "we," and "our." To inspire people to attend hearings, it is vital that you make individuals feel responsible for the fate of your community.

The timing of the notice is also important. Notices should be in people's mailboxes a week before the public hearing. Notify your members so that they have enough time to make room in their schedules for the meeting. But beware of notifying so far in advance that your allies forget about the meeting altogether by the time it comes along.

In addition to the written notice, your communications committee should use its telephone tree to call every member in your organization two to three days before the public hearing as a reminder to attend. Remember, telephoning your membership can double or triple the turnout at any meeting. People appreciate the personal gesture of a neighbor calling to remind them of an important meeting.

Why is a large crowd so important at public hearings? Because politicians respond to numbers. After all, every person at a public hearing represents a vote. Moreover, politicians' careers depend on their popularity with their constituents. So if you make it clear by your numbers at the meeting that their political careers may depend on their decision on a particular issue, politicians are more likely to pay attention to what you say.

Your organization may have an excellent president. You may like to believe that if she shows up with only three or four representatives from your group that politicians will perk up and listen to her because she is so well informed and sincere. Forget it! That's the path to defeat!

No matter how persuasive your leadership, at public hearings it is the numbers that count. Your president is only as powerful as the crowd of people sitting behind her in the audience. Your president has power because the polticians realize that she speaks for many people and that those people care enough to show up at hearings.

This law of numbers holds true for large and small issues. At public hearings, always have a crowd on your side. For a relatively minor public hearing on a minor issue, still have no fewer than ten people there who are prepared to speak. This is true even if you know in advance that public officials are on your side and certain to vote in your favor. Even if the politicians are your bosom buddies, you must provide them with ample public testimony as sufficient reason to vote in your behalf.

Can too many hearings exhaust your membership? Yes, they can. Your opposition might actually enjoy scheduling lots of public hearings in the hope that with every meeting fewer of your members will show up to oppose him. To avoid this attrition, you need to keep your membership enthusiastic so that with every meeting more people attend. Keep your cause in the limelight through letters to the editor in your local newspapers. Constant exposure in the press will continue to recruit new members for your organization while it keeps the old members energized.

Preparing and Making Your Presentation

Prepare speeches.   Members of your organization should prepare written speeches. Never rely on volunteers from the audience to speak extemporaneously on your behalf. Only a few people dare to do this. Although effective in their own dramatic way, they will probably deliver more emotion than substance.

You can put your organization's prepared speeches to further good use by revising them as letters to the editor for your local newspapers.

Rehearse the speeches.   Most people are not accustomed to public speaking. Many have a phobia about speaking in front of a crowd. To allay this fear, arrange for rehearsals a week or two before the public hearing. If you have a lot of speakers, divide them into two or three groups and have them read their speeches to one another over coffee and cake in the relaxed atmosphere of a neighbor's living room. This gives each speaker some feedback on his or her speech, and any errors may be caught in advance. Rehearsals also create a wonderful camaraderie among your speakers. Usually only one rehearsal is necessary.

Prepare a document combining all of your speakers' concerns.   Before the public hearing, collect and compile all of your speakers' written speeches and present this as your organization's written commentary on the environmental review. This document should be well organized and neatly typed. Copies of this document should be distributed to the planning department, city council, and to each significant public official and commission.

In addition, at the time of the hearing, each individual speaker should give to the appropriate official a separate typed copy of his or her own speech to become part of the documented testimony on the project. Whenever possible, individuals' commentaries should be mailed to the commission or board in advance of the hearing itself.

Time limitation.   Many city councils and public commissions impose a time restriction on public testimony. For example, individuals may have only three to five minutes to present their points of view. The presidents of organizations usually are permitted more time since they are addressing the concerns of an entire organization. So always find out how long you have to speak before a public hearing and prepare your speech accordingly.

If you have more to say than the time restriction permits, your written statement to public officials will cover those issues. Officials are supposed to read these written statements as part of the public testimony documentation. However, it may be important that all of your speech be read aloud at the public hearing. If so, then divide your speech in half, deliver the first section yourself, and ask a friend to present the second part.

Avoid repetition.   Each of your speakers should address different key issues. If all of your speakers focus on the same concerns, public officials are likely to request that only those who bring up new points may speak. So assign different topics to your speakers beforehand. There is generally a myriad of items to discuss at any public hearing: geology, traffic, toxics, safety, noise, air pollution, wildlife, wetlands, trees, groundwater, precedents, legal issues, planning policy, alternatives, social and economic impacts, etc. Address every angle.

Visual aids.   Visual aids help make your speech memorable. If you are protesting a proposed toxic dump or ugly industrial site, show photographs of existing ones. Compare them with photographs of the beautiful site today. Before and after photos are dramatic. Enlarge photographs so that a room full of people can appreciate your visual statement.

If you are opposing a proposed nuclear power plant, for example, enlarge photographs of the disasters at Three-Mile Island and Chernobyl. Or if oil drilling is proposed off your coastline, prepare large photographs of the ecological devastation from offshore oil spills in Alaska, California, Texas, and elsewhere.

Positive commentary.   An essential part of any environmental review is the question of what alternatives exist to the proposed project. This is your chance to provide positive comments. You may praise the existing site as it now stands as the best of all alternatives—the wetlands are best left as wetlands; the forest is best left intact; the city neighborhood is best unchanged; let the ranches be. Discuss all the advantages—environmental, social, and economic—of preserving the site as it is today. You may also suggest alternatives that include various enhancements of the environmental qualities of the site in question, such as transforming the land to a public park or open space.

Stay cool. No yelling.   Emotions will be running high at the public hearing. Your group will be nervous and scared. The politicians' heartbeats will be thumping loudly too when they see all your supporters in the audience. Your opposition, their lawyers, and lobbyists will likely be in the audience giving you the evil eye. Stay cool.

The more rational your speeches, the more you will impress the politicians, planners, and commissioners. They have heard more than their share of incoherent citizens complaining about everything from potholes in the local roads to a neighbor's tree falling into another neighbor's yard and injuring the family dog.

A well-orchestrated, well-researched presentation will accomplish much more than any spontaneous ranting can possibly do. Ranters are generally viewed as crackpots by politicians and commissioners. Emotion in lieu of facts diminishes your effectiveness. However, an emotional style of delivery of solid facts makes for dramatic, memorable presentations.

A successful finale.   If, at the finale of the public hearing, the officials vote in favor of your side, you may feel like applauding. Go right ahead! Applaud yourselves, your victory, and the democratic process!

With every public hearing, you forge the future of your community. The theater of grassroots activism will include moments of drama, comedy, heroics, and suspense in the continuous battle of opposing sides. So celebrate your victorious public hearings. Throw a party for your allies. Take a long, triumphant stroll on the land you just saved. Savor your success! You earned it!

You recognized an environmental problem. You began a grassroots organization to solve it. You researched the issues. You learned how to use the democratic process. You networked with other environmental groups. You met with public officials and informed them about your concerns. You produced impressive newsletters and educated your community. You flooded the newspapers with letters to the editor and inspired reporters to cover your cause. At the public hearings, all of your grassroots organizing culminated in victory for your side. Bravo! You have become an influential power in your community to save the environment.

However, you will soon discover that the struggle to preserve the environment has become a lifelong project, an enduring passion. For example, the particular issue to which you have dedicated yourself may take years to resolve. Many more public hearings may await you, plus years of community political organizing. Moreover, you will find yourself committed to ever new environmental challenges.

As an individual, your abilities will expand; as an activist, your community influence will grow; as an environmentalist, you will master the democratic process to make our planet a better world.

PART II

How to Win Environmental Campaigns and Elect Environmentalists to Public Office

CHAPTER 7

How to Win Grassroots Elections

Y our local politicians make all the difference in the world to your community. If your local city council members and county supervisors truly did represent your city's values, then you could spend more time sipping cool drinks in a hammock while applauding your elected officials, who are busy speaking out for you. Indeed, those politicians who do fight for the environment and social justice deserve our heartfelt praise and support. But alas, how few of our elected officials do speak for us! In fact, many grassroots activists spend most of their time fighting disastrous environmental decisions made by local politicians. Therefore, it is one of the most important tasks of grassroots activism to place our own representatives in public office.

Why Grassroots Activism?

Grassroots activism usually springs up in a community as an act of rebellion, not only against specific environmental and development problems, but also against local politicians who refuse to do anything about the problems. It takes only a few months of grassroots involvement in your community to realize that all too often your elected officials are the problem. Environmental organizations have grown in leaps and bounds over the last years, and many ecologists credit this explosion of environmental activism as a rebellion against the politicians who repeatedly vote for the special interests of big business against the welfare of the people and the environment.

The grassroots movement is also an antidote to the cynicism that has overtaken our national political scene. National elections remain out of the control of average citizens. Presidential, gubernatorial, and senatorial campaigns are run by a phalanx of professional movers and shakers who raise and spend millions of dollars on slick, often misleading campaigns. Serious social, economic, and environmental issues have been reduced to simplistic "sound bites" for television consumption. The American public has grown disillusioned with political campaign practices. The fact that fewer than 50 percent of our population vote in national elections—the lowest voter turnout of any world democracy—signals the profound crisis of our political system.

Grassroots campaigns, however, give the power back to the people. After all, the word *democracy* means "rule of the people." Originally from Greek terms, *demos* means "people" and *kratos* translates to "rule" or "power." Democracy literally signifies power to the people! On the local level, this political power is there for the taking.

The satisfaction and rewards of grassroots activism are truly open to everyone. Let's say that you have never been involved in any political campaign in your life. You may be in awe of the whole mysterious process. Let me reassure you that at the local level election campaigns are neither mysterious nor difficult. I have seen successful campaigns organized by schoolteachers, bus drivers, football coaches, security guards, secretaries, carpenters, architects, dentists, realtors, plumbers, students, homemakers, ranchers, waitresses, farmers, nurses, engineers, physicians, scientists, musicians, flight attendants, socialites, firemen, fishermen, artists, and every other profession. None of these people had any political experience before their grassroots involvement in their community; yet they organized strategic political campaigns in their hometowns and succeeded in putting environmentally aware candidates into local political office. All of these people would agree that their involvement in grassroots political campaigns was one of the most exciting times of their lives.

Grassroots organizing is an antidote to voter apathy. In local elections, voter turnout is often less than in national elections. Many people in a community are not even aware that a local election is taking place although they may have noticed a few signs by the roadside telling them to vote for some candidate or other for some office or other. But they think, "Who cares? My vote doesn't make any difference. All politicians are the same anyway. So why vote?" How tragic! Without grassroots activism, your adversaries win elections—and without a fight!

Still, democracy is not dead, only dormant, like Sleeping Beauty waiting for a grassroots activist to awaken her with a caring kiss. The excitement of grassroots activism lies in the tremendous democratic power that is waiting for you to embrace it. You *can* make a difference. You can determine the future of your community. Your city's destiny is in your hands. You only need to reach for it.

The Rewards of Grassroots Activism

The rewards of grassroots activism are threefold. First, you awaken to your own power to change your world. Second, you teach your neighbors of their ability to make a difference. Third, you actually succeed in electing environmentally responsible people who preserve and protect the beauty and health of your part of the planet. The satisfaction of these accomplishments is hard to beat.

Keep in mind that the few months that you spend working on a political campaign can save you years of grief in the long run. For example, one community, which was environmentally savvy, had a majority on the city council who were conservationists. Election time came around. The incumbent environmentalists were certain of victory, so their supporters ran a low-key campaign and many did not even vote because they were so confident that their candidates would win reelection. Well, to everyone's horror, the good guys lost. The victorious were three little-known but hard-campaigning candidates who pretended in their campaign rhetoric to represent "the people." As it turned out, the only people whom they represented were developers.

As a result of the environmentalists' cocky overconfidence the community spent four years fighting virtually every decision of the new city council majority. The council approved every kind of housing and commercial development project, ignoring the hundreds of angry residents who spoke at city council meetings. The new city council members soon became hardened to public criticism and turned deaf ears to the furious harangues and tearful pleas made at public hearings.

The result was four years of citizen initiatives and referendums to overturn the council's decisions, as well as costly lawsuits to reverse the council's dreadful actions. By the end of those four years of political battles, the community was exhausted. They had managed to stop many of the city council's worst efforts, but at a tremendous price! Not only did they have to raise thousands of dollars to pay for referendum campaigns and legal fees, but they were also forced to spend myriad anguished hours at political meetings instead of relaxing at home with their families.

The moral of the story is: Every election is an important election. Get involved. Campaign hard. Fight to win. Your community's future depends on you.

Remember, no one is born with an intuitive knowledge of how to fight a successful political campaign. It's something everyone must learn from scratch. So if you have no political campaign experience, join the crowd. During our first steps into the political arena, we all begin naive as a newborn babe.

This chapter and those that follow are designed for everyone who is working on a political campaign—from the candidate to the campaign manager to the office volunteer who comes in to campaign headquarters once a week to answer the telephone. It is important that everyone in a campaign understand the big picture and the little details of an election. The recommendations on how to run a campaign are essential for the novice but equally important for the experienced campaigner. As I have witnessed in my own community, even professional politicians can run costly, inefficient, and ineffective campaigns. Even popular incumbents make devastating campaign decisions that can lose elections for them.

The information that follows will help you run a successful campaign no matter what your experience, your location, or your campaign issues. Merely adapt the general principles to your city, your candidate, and your concerns. The basics of running an effective grassroots campaign are similar everywhere.

First, you need a candidate.

The Candidate

Running for Office Yourself

Are you the candidate? Don't laugh! You may be just the right person to be your next city council member, mayor, or county supervisor. If you have been an active member of your community—let's say on your school board, in your housing association, or in environmental associations—people may start telling you: "By the way, you're such a resourceful organizer, you always have such constructive ideas, and you care so much about our town. Have you ever considered running for office?"

The first time someone asks you this question, you may chuckle and reply that political office is the furthest thing from your mind. But if you hear this question from a second and then a third person, the idea may begin to strike a chord in you. Then you should seriously consider running for office.

Some people plan for years to run for a local office. Some decide to run on the spur of the moment. The essential is to have the proper experience to prove to the voters that you can handle the job.

The long-range approach is exemplified by Marsha, a thirty-eight-year-old woman who moved to a small Oregon community from Boston with her husband and young children. After years of a stressful, fast-paced job on the East Coast, she settled down to the domestic life of a homemaker in her rustic new town, hoping for peace and quiet. But within a few years, she found herself loving her new neighborhood so much that she became involved in a series of local environmental battles.

One of her friends, a grassroots candidate for city council, asked her to be his campaign manager. She accepted. He won the election. Even though the campaign had been difficult, the political bug had bitten Marsha. A few friends asked her if she had ever considered running for office. She denied it, but privately she began to think seriously about it.

After four years in town, Marsha realized that she was still considered a newcomer in Oregon, an outsider, whose strong Boston accent stressed her foreign origins. People in her town were not wild about outsiders. Rightly, Marsha knew that she had to gain experience in how her town operated politically and to prove herself to local activists. Secretly planning to run for the next city council election in two years, she put herself through an intensive training course. She participated in the activities of every environmental organization in town. She joined her housing association, the school association, and the parks commission. She quickly became part of the leadership of every organization she joined.

When it came time for the next city council election, Marsha had proven herself an ardent activist and had an impressive list of credentials of public service, plus allies who happened to be the Who's Who of her community's most popular environmental leaders. She won the election for city council and eventually became mayor, fighting for environmental causes every inch of the way.

This methodical, intensive approach works, but many of you may have accumulated much experience and many allies without even realizing it. Perhaps you naturally have been involved in issues and organizations in your community for years. You love your town and you naturally like being involved.

You may already have all the credentials and experience you need to run for office.

The decision to run may be spur of the moment. Some people have never thought of running for office in their lives, yet an election comes along, and a few months later they find themselves in public office.

For example, Bill had lived in Illinois most of his life. He was an attorney by profession, but his passion was fishing. Through his love of fishing, he found himself thrust into many wildlife organizations, which led to his involvement in campaigns to save rivers and lakes from pollution.

Bill was distraught when he heard that no one was going to challenge a popular mayor who was running for his fourth term in office. In two of the last three elections, the incumbent had run unopposed. Although charming, handsome, and silver-tongued, the politician was a strong ally of oil and chemical companies who always made hefty contributions to his campaigns. Bill's efforts to save Illinois' rivers and lakes from pollution always met with opposition from this politician.

Bill frantically called activist friends to urge them to run for office. Friends claimed to be too bogged down in personal problems to even consider it. "Besides," everyone said, "the mayor can't lose. He's too entrenched in office. He has too many powerful supporters."

Desperate, Bill went to city hall requesting forms to run for office himself. No one thought Bill had the slightest chance of winning the election. With no idea how to run a campaign, Bill hired a professional campaign manager with a good track record of ousting incumbents. The public found Bill competent because he was an attorney and likable because of his love of fishing. But he was still relatively unknown, and he had paltry campaign funds compared to the wealthy incumbent. Yet in a surprise upset, Bill won the election.

With little to say about his own political accomplishments, Bill's campaign stressed the corrupt practices of the incumbent, who had reigned unchallenged for years. Although voters weren't too sure who Bill was, they were certain that the incumbent had deceived them long enough. Once aware of the cor-

ruption, the public demanded a change. Bill, who had begun planning his retirement only the previous year, found himself as mayor of his city, doing everything possible to protect his precious rivers and lakes.

Bill and Marsha are only two of the innumerable individuals who are now shaping their communities' future thanks to grassroots activism. You could be next. If you are pondering the possibility of running for office, make a few telephone calls to friends. Tell them your idea and get their reactions. If most of them grow excited about the notion of you in office, then you are off to a good start. Ask some local activists and former and current office-holders for their reactions. If people are generally enthusiastic about your running for office, then go for it! You have already collected some likely volunteers for your campaign.

Note: Don't be discouraged if you lose your first campaign. It may take more than one campaign to place you into political office. Take Alan, for example. Alan was a grassroots activist in Florida. A high school teacher by profession, he dreamed of running for the state legislature. In fact, he ran twice and lost twice. However, his dream never faded.

A city council election came up, and Alan decided that through his two previous state legislature campaigns, he had gained enough notoriety in his hometown to win a city council election. He was right. In two successive elections he enjoyed two stunning victories and became a popular, well-respected city councilman. But he never forgot his dream. After eight years on the city council, he again ran for the state legislature. This time he won. His years on the city council had brought him the extra campaign experience, government know-how, and countywide fame to win the state seat.

Alan may have started out his political career losing elections, but he never felt defeated. His years as a high school athletics coach gave him great fighting spirit. His motto should become your motto: Never give up!

Supporting a Candidate

Perhaps you have no desire at all to run for public office, but you enjoy working as an activist for various causes. What's more, you realize that it is essential to have people with an environmental conscience in public office. Then you will be looking eagerly for other candidates to support.

In local elections, you have a good opportunity to get to know the candidates personally. You become acquainted with the candidate's spouse, children, moods, habits, and temperament. You may learn more about the candidate than you want to know. Maybe you don't like the way he spoils his children; his bragging about their achievements gets on your nerves. His arrogant, brassy, bossy tone may irritate you. Nonetheless, he may have proven himself a tireless environmental activist, successfully leading grassroots campaigns to save the major parks in your city from high-rise development proposals.

Always set aside your personal assessment of the candidate's private peccadillos. You want a good candidate, not a saint. Besides, some of the traits that may make for a good politician—being assertive and outspoken—may not be your ideal for a best friend. But you are not choosing a best friend, nor will the voters be selecting the perfect human being.

One city councilman told me, "Why would a grown adult want to take all this abuse from the public? It's like setting oneself up in a carnival booth as a target for people to knock down with baseball bats." Holding public office is not easy. A politician is always at the center of some controversy, always being yelled at by some sector of the community. At any given time, 50 percent of the population is likely to be furious with a politician. You want your candidates to be tough, decisive, and especially loyal to their environmental principles no matter how much pressure is put on them to abandon their beliefs.

Your community is asking a lot of its candidates. So if they irritate you in minor ways, you simply must focus on what you admire about them. Your candidates are going to be fighting tooth and nail for your environmental values. That is a lot to ask of anybody. So be tolerant of other weaknesses and foibles in their characters.

Do, however, beware of supporting a candidate whose life has been simply too scandalous for your community to accept. What may happen in such a situation is that your candidate's private life may overshadow the real election issues. Your opposition will rarely hesitate to advertise the fact that your candidate is a known alcoholic or tax evader.

For example, a certain city council candidate in Texas ran on the "big business means progress" ticket. He was all for growth and development and, quite naturally, indifferent to environmental issues. The chamber of commerce loved him. However, through their research on him, the environmental forces in town discovered that in his college days the candidate had run a short-lived business to sell hydroponic gardening equipment to marijuana growers.

The environmental clique gleefully leaked documents to the local press proving the "big business" candidate's past involvement with marijuana enterprises. The press picked up the story, and the candidate's credibility was instantly flushed down the toilet. Of course, the irony is that the environmental group would never have condemned the fellow for his past hydroponic business, but they knew that the conservatives in town would sooner see such a man strung up than elected to office.

So always be cognizant of what idiosyncrasies your community can accept. Some communities have a remarkably high tolerance. For example, in Sausalito, California, an infamous former madam became a prominent city council member. Sally Stanford had retired from her lucrative bordello business in San Francisco to open a posh restaurant across the bay in Sausalito. Sally grew civic-minded (in her business she had grown to know many politicians very, very well) and developed a passion for Sausalito issues. She cared deeply about her community and ran for Sausalito city council until she finally won—and later even became mayor. Sausalito is a small, picturesque city containing many trendy, well-heeled, well-traveled people who are proud of their liberal spirit. If Sally needed more than one campaign to win an election, it was not because of public prejudice against her past profession. Sally ran on the issues and won because of her position on the issues.

Such examples abound in the South, which has a history of eccentric politicians with scandalous private lives who nonetheless became popular political leaders. Louisiana's Huey and Earl Long were outrageous personalities who managed long political careers.

All depends on the priorities of your own neighbors. Make certain that you understand your community's values. If your candidate offends those values, he or she is almost guaranteed to lose the election.

Democrat or Republican?

Grassroots environmental action is often nonpartisan. The preservation of old-growth forests, public beaches, mountain ridgelines, deserts, wildlife, or clean water overrides party distinctions. People either value nature and quality of life or they don't. Party affiliation has nothing to do with this love.

To win in local elections, it is essential to stress your community's issues so intensely that the candidate's particular party simply does not matter to the voters. Many of you will be surprised how well Democrats and Republicans get along in environmental campaigns. Initially, it seems contradictory to Democrats that ardent Republicans would support wildlife causes. Moreover, diehard Republicans are stunned that their new, admirable friends turn out to be Democrats. Soon party lines lose their meaning.

In some communities with a large Republican majority, Democratic candidates can win local elections because they stress the issues in campaigns, not their party. It's a strange fact that many Republicans who devoutly vote the party ticket in national elections may vote solely for Democrats in local elections. The opposite can also happen, where Democrats vote for ecology-minded Republicans on the local scene.

Whereas national elections too often are based on superficial party rhetoric, local elections remain the true arena where vital issues can be debated. When key issues are stressed in local elections, many voters literally couldn't care less about the party of the candidates—even if they belong to alternative political parties. Whatever your candidate's political persuasion, you must make your community's hot environmental concerns the election issues. That is what will excite and unite the voters.

So before beginning your campaign, put away all your preconceived notions of what makes an environmentally concerned person. They come in all shapes and sizes. You will be working on campaigns alongside all kinds of people with the goal of reaching all kinds of voters.

For example, one of the most ardent nature lovers I know recently enlisted in the U.S. Marines. He loves the life of a Marine but is dismayed at the garbage that seafaring Marines toss carelessly overboard and is making this pollution of the oceans his cause.

Another example of a surprise ally is Admiral G. R. LaRocque, who founded the center for Defense Information in Washington, D.C., in 1972. Admiral LaRocque has devoted himself to achieving world peace through military cooperation rather than confrontation. He is an outspoken advocate of nuclear disarmament. No one would expect an admiral to be such a dedicated peace activist, but so it goes. Peace activists and environmentalists come in every variety.

The moral is: Expect allies from unexpected places. Let your campaign accentuate what you all have in common.

Recalls, Referendums, and Initiatives

There are all kinds of elections. Your upcoming election may not be about a candidate's campaign, but about a campaign to recall an elected official because of inappropriate conduct, or a campaign for a referendum to reverse a city council decision, or a campaign for an initiative to establish an environmental law.

Recalls, referendums, and initiatives are divided into two distinct phases. First, a certain amount of signatures must be gathered on a petition to permit the recall, referendum, or initiative to appear on the ballot. Once the issue qualifies for the ballot, then the second phase involves the actual campaign to win the election.

In order to write up a legally binding petition and to collect the right number of signatures, you must contact your city, county, and state governments to obtain all the proper instructions. Booklets are available. Ask the clerk at city hall for assistance. Your city clerk is likely to provide you with helpful material and can direct you where to look for further guidance. At the state level, contact the offices of the state attorney general or the secretary of state to request all the information necessary. Be aware that laws are constantly being revised on these matters. So collect the most up-to-date information.

In addition, it is advisable to submit your petition to an experienced environmental lawyer to check that the wording on the petition falls within legal parameters. A dedicated environmental attorney will usually charge a minimum fee for such a service.

After you have collected enough signatures to qualify your

issue for the ballot, your campaign will be run much the same as if you were campaigning for a candidate. Only it is the issue—the recall, the referendum, or the initiative—that takes the place of the candidate. Accordingly, you can use the recommendations in the following chapters for these kinds of campaigns too.

After you have chosen a candidate, what's next? How do you get your candidate elected to public office? Read on. The next chapters will provide a clear guide to victory.

CHAPTER 8

🌲

The Campaign Committee

E very campaign is a team effort. The candidate may be the one whose name is flashed on signs around town, the one whose face smiles in newspaper photographs, the one who is debating opponents in front of cheering crowds. But it is thanks to the campaign workers that the candidate catches the public's eye at all.

Warren Nelson, who captured the mayor's seat in the small town of Yountville, California, nestled in Napa Valley's wine country, likes to joke how he won the election in his town of fewer than 3000 people: "All I had to do was visit my favorite restaurant, climb up on a chair, announce my candidacy, and shake hands with all my friends. Who says campaigning is hard work?"

Warren's charming self-effacing humor downplays the tremendous amount of work that he and his campaign volunteers put into winning the mayor's seat in even a small, peaceful community. For although Warren's main goal was to create more public parks for his town, even this noble end met with opposition and controversy. There is no place too small for controversy or grassroots activism.

Every campaign, whether in a cozy town or a bustling metropolis, needs loyal, dedicated grassroots volunteers, including:

* a hard-working campaign director
* a capable treasurer and fundraiser
* organizers to throw the kick-off party
* a letters-to-the-editor committee
* a telephone committee
* a good political writer to draft newspaper ads, mailers, and press releases
* researchers to dig out facts about the opposition and the campaign issues
* shopping-center staffers to pass out campaign information
* precinct walkers to go door to door with campaign brochures
* a committee responsible for putting up campaign signs

Certainly there is a great deal of overlap in campaign duties. Every grassroots volunteer soon learns to be a jack-of-all-trades. The qualities and responsibilities of the campaign director are the subject of the rest of this chapter. The duties of the campaign treasurer are discussed in Chapter Nine and those of other volunteers in Chapter Twelve.

The Volunteer Campaign Director

A good campaign director is someone with the following qualities.

* *Someone with time.*   Campaign director is a difficult job. I have had several candidates ask me to be their campaign director by pouring honey on the job description. "Oh, it won't be much work. Just a few hours on your weekends." Don't you believe it! Being a campaign director is a big responsibility. A person with a separate full-time job must be prepared to put in long evenings and weekends on the telephone and at strategy

meetings. So you need an energetic volunteer who has the time to devote several months to the campaign.

• *Someone with experience.* Naturally, a volunteer with campaign experience is ideal. But political experience is not necessary. One of the best grassroots campaigns I have seen was run by a city council candidate, a school principal who selected a teacher as his campaign director. The teacher had no campaign experience whatsoever, but as a teacher she was an expert organizer and communicator. The campaign was smoothly run and very successful. Compared to a classroom of rowdy students, a political campaign is a piece of cake. So, for lack of an experienced campaigner, look for character traits in a person that indicate the promise of a good campaign director.

• *Someone who can keep a wild group together.* Unlike other environmental organizations that exist over a period of years and have time to develop a smoothly functioning team, a campaign committee for a local election may exist for only a few months. A political campaign throws all kinds of people together for a short, intense time. The committee volunteers come from all over your community and have a variety of personalities and priorities. The campaign director must be able to deal with a room full of strong egos and opinions. She must be able to keep them unified with her vision constantly on the objective of winning the election. This is not easy. I have witnessed more than one campaign director, male and female, reduced to tears by their committee's own dissension.

A campaign director for an environmental candidate once confided to me, "Every meeting is a nightmare. Nobody can agree on anything." Nonetheless, that particular campaign led to a terrific victory. Despite personality differences, the campaign committee was still able to coordinate sound strategies.

• *Someone who enjoys controversy.* The campaign director must be able to control the controversies within the campaign committee. Volunteers will be throwing out all kinds of ideas for action. She must be able to steer your committee to cooperate in order to actualize the best of these ideas. She also must be willing to use controversial issues to put your opponent up against the ropes. This is not a job for someone who thinks campaigning is a cordial tea party.

• *Someone with a strong stomach.*   Your objective is to win the election. Political campaigns are a tough business. A campaign director is much like a football coach, who must deal with the opposition's illegal tackling and a wide assortment of violations, all committed when the referee is not looking. Dirty tricks known to any football fan are child's play in comparison to political practices. Like a coach, the campaign director must be willing to use every fair offense and defense to score goals.

A wishy-washy coach, just like a genteel campaigner, is doomed to defeat. This is not a recommendation to use deceit or lies in a campaign. On the contrary, you must rely solely on the truth to win your campaign.

Here's an example of how a genteel campaign can lose the election. Two popular environmental candidates were running for city council in Minnesota. Overconfident about victory, their campaign directors ran lackluster, low-key campaigns. The anticonservation forces ran an aggressive attack against the environmentalists, mailing out brochures full of lies. The environmentalists' campaign directors decided foolishly that it was below their dignity to respond to the outrageous lies of the opposition. These campaign directors pronounced loftily that the voters were too smart to be deceived by such obvious lies. Well, since the voters never heard any rebuttal to the lies, they simply believed them. The popular environmentalists lost the election and dropped out of politics, much to the detriment of their community.

Deceitful political practices, such as lies, false rumors, back-stabbing, and double-crossing, should never be employed. But this treachery must always be revealed in strong, clear terms when you discover your opposition using it. The voter will not be able to discern that your opposition is telling lies unless your campaign reveals the truth.

In addition, reality will usually provide you with plenty of hard-hitting truths against your opponent. Your campaign director must be willing to use these truths for everything that they are worth to educate the public on the important issues. A good campaign director needs work gloves, not white gloves.

• *Someone with the fighting underdog spirit.*   Even if your candidate is a popular favorite, your campaign committee must organize as if he were the underdog with everything against him. Nothing loses a campaign more quickly than complacency. Many incumbents and popular favorites have lost elections because they felt cocksure of victory. No matter the popularity of your candidate, always take for granted that your candidate could lose.

I recall one city council election where an unknown homemaker ran against a favored environmentalist incumbent. The incumbent's campaign never took the homemaker seriously with her homemade signs and simplistic campaign slogans. However, the homemaker won the election because she campaigned harder than any other candidate. The ecology in-crowd did not take her seriously. But the voters did.

Underdogs have the edge in their hunger, their strong drive to win. Entrenched in political office, incumbents tend to lose that hunger. It is a campaign director's duty to keep alive that keen desire for victory.

• *Someone to lead your campaign committee to win every aspect of the campaign.*   To run the best campaign possible, you must do the following:

1. Have more letters to the editor printed in the newspapers than your opposition.

2. Win the public debates. You must fill every audience with your allies to cheer loudly for your candidate.

3. Have more signs than your opposition on display throughout your entire community. Also, your candidate's signs should be up first.

4. Have the most effective mailers.

5. Determine the issues of the campaign from the very beginning and throughout the entire campaign.

6. Always be on the aggressive. Voters perceive defensiveness as weakness.

7. Have volunteers at shopping centers passing out brochures for your candidate.

8. Have a telephone committee calling your supporters to remind them to vote just before election day.

Remember, your campaign director and committee volunteers need not be superbeings. The essential ingredient is their deep caring for the campaign and the issues. From this caring, all the other necessary qualities for a successful campaign will emerge.

The Professional Campaign Director

Do you need to hire a professional campaign director? A dedicated, competent volunteer, even without experience, can make the best campaign director. She cares deeply and will work hard. She knows her community and its issues. On the other hand, it is important to keep in mind that many professional campaign directors are political mercenaries who work for whatever side happens to be paying them at the moment. This year it may be your side, next year it may be your opposition's. That is simply the nature of their profession. However, there certainly are some good professional campaign directors out there. So, for lack of a suitable volunteer, you may want to hire a professional.

How do you find a good professional campaign director? Don't look in the Yellow Pages! Ask for referrals from environmental organizations and other allies.

When interviewing people for the job of campaign director, ask to see press clippings of their previous victories. They should possess a track record of victories in elections in communities similar to yours. A big-city campaign director or someone used to working in your state capital may be com-

pletely inappropriate for your suburban community. He may not understand suburban concerns nor your particular community's style. Someone accustomed to campaigning in suburban areas might use campaign tactics that are offensive to rural communities. If you are trying to oust an incumbent, you might look for a campaign director experienced in bouncing incumbents out of office. Since environmental issues are the key focus of your campaign, seek someone who has successfully fought in environmental campaigns.

How much do you pay a professional campaign director? The fee varies enormously. Here are three examples concerning one particular campaign director. In one city, a candidate from a wealthy family gave the campaign director $100,000 to get her elected to the board of supervisors. With this money, fancy billboards were erected and lots of expensive mailers were sent out. In spite of the fortune spent on the campaign, the woman lost the election because the voters simply did not agree with her position on the issues.

In a neighboring smaller city, another candidate hired this same campaign director for a city council election and paid him a $15,000 fee out of his own pocket. Not well known in his community, this particular candidate had very few volunteers working on his campaign, so he focused on mailers. The campaign director researched and wrote a series of mailers that were brutal attacks against the incumbent, pointing out his inconsistent policies and using the incumbent's own public statements and voting record against him. The blitz of mailers succeeded brilliantly. The little-known underdog won. Eventually, his subsequent fundraising events reimbursed his initial $15,000 expense.

In the third case, a well-known and much liked city council candidate hired the same professional campaign director and paid him $5000. This popular candidate was able to pay this fee entirely from campaign contributions. She had many volunteers working on her campaign and ran every campaign committee meeting by herself, without the hired campaign director's presence. She used the professional primarily to do all her campaign writing (newspaper ads, press releases, mailers, ballot statements, kick-off party invitations, etc.). Furthermore, as a long-time grassroots activist, this candidate had been involved in so many controversies over the years that she counted on the professional to keep her focused on the most important issues of the moment. This environmental candidate won a tremendous victory.

The lessons learned from the three above-mentioned cases are useful. First, be creative and flexible in how you use the professional. Adapt him to your needs. Outline your requirements in your contract with him. Second, remember, you need not pay a fortune to win a grassroots election.

CHAPTER 9

Campaign Fundraising and the Kick-off Party

E ven in an all-volunteer campaign, an election costs money. You may be spared having to pay for a staff of campaign workers, but inevitably you need money for newspaper ads, mailers, bumperstickers, and signs. These items tend to cost more in larger cities than in smaller towns, primarily because in larger cities you must deal with a bigger population and therefore more mailers, more signs, and more bumperstickers. Moreover, the larger the city, the more its newspaper advertising tends to cost. But even in small towns, campaign costs are escalating all the time.

If you have never been involved in a campaign before, the thought of raising and spending thousands of dollars probably sends shivers up your spine. But don't let fundraising fears keep you from pursuing your goals of winning the election. Once you start looking around your community, you will be amazed at the sources of fundraising right in your own backyard.

The heart of grassroots fundraising is your appeal to the average citizen for contributions. Individuals will donate $10, $25, $50, $100, or more to your campaign. These donations can add up to a considerable war chest.

Grassroots fundraising differs from traditional fundraising

by politicians, who seek contributions from influential businesses and organizations that can afford to donate thousands of dollars. In fact, these days, none of us is terribly surprised when we hear of senators or presidents deeply indebted for their political victories to oil companies, the automobile industry, steel manufacturers, developers, and corporations tied to the military.

However, many voters do not yet realize that even on a local level politicians may have sold out completely to their contributors before they even take office. In all likelihood, many of your local politicians have made numerous promises, tacitly or openly, to the biggest businesses in your area—all to loosen campaign dollars from personal and corporate pockets. These politicians are indebted, and their decisions in office often reflect this indebtedness.

The beauty of grassroots fundraising is that individuals are donating money to your campaign because they believe in the same things that you do. You are not burdened with gratitude to any particular financial donor. You remain free to vote your conscience when you take office.

The Kick-off Party

The kick-off party is your first opportunity to collect thousands of dollars in campaign contributions. It can also be a lot of fun.

What is a kick-off party? It is a festive occasion for celebrating a person's candidacy. Let's assume you are the candidate. Your supporters pay to come. Your sponsors provide the food and drink. Everyone eats, drinks, and makes merry. You give your first speech of the campaign, and an auction earns thousands of dollars for your campaign coffers.

Finding Sponsors

The first thing to do in planning your kick-off party is to attract sponsors. These sponsors will be the first contributors to your campaign. Each sponsor agrees to donate a specific minimum sum, such as $25 or $50. In addition, sponsors volunteer to supply your kick-off party with food and drinks, plus items to auction. In short, your sponsors will donate everything necessary to create a great kick-off party so that all the money you collect at the party may be used directly for your campaign needs, such as signs, ads, and mailers.

You may find your sponsors by mail or by telephone.

Mailings are a common way of finding sponsors. The first mailer of your campaign will be an announcement of your candidacy to fifty or more people who are likely to support your candidacy. If you were active in various groups—housing associations, environmental organizations, school committees, civic clubs, etc.—then the members of these associations are your first targets for the sponsorship mailer. Membership lists can be obtained from the organizations' presidents or secretaries. Sometimes the organization will gladly supply computer-generated, peel-off address labels.

This first letter should be printed on your official campaign stationery. The letterhead should display your name, campaign slogan, address, and telephone number. For example:

Joan Doright for City Council Campaign
333 Tree Street
Greenville, Iowa
(333) 333-3333

or

Bob Forest Campaign
SLOW GROWTH FOR OUR TOWN
11 Grass Lane
Woodland, Vermont
(111) 111-1111

The letter should answer the following questions: What office are you running for? Why are you running for office? What issues and principles do you stand for? What do you hope to accomplish if elected? What are your credentials?

After your succinct one-page letter answers all the above

questions, it should make an appeal for sponsors. In many communities, sponsors for city council or county supervisor candidates are asked to contribute $25, $35, or $50, sometimes even more. To find out what sponsorship fee your community will respond to positively, check with candidates from previous campaigns in your area. What did they request as a sponsor's contribution? If you ask too little, people assume that you are not worth more. If you ask too much, people simply may not be able to afford it.

Following is a sample letter:

Len Seashore Campaign for State Assembly
SAVE OUR BAY
555 Fishtail Road
Lobstercove, Massachusetts
(222) 222-2222

Dear Friends and Neighbors:

I am running for the State Assembly and need your help to be elected. For years now we have witnessed our State Assembly vote repeatedly against our interests. We have seen factory after factory built in our community pouring their toxic waste into our bay. As a result, our fishing industry, the backbone of our community, has been poisoned. Fishermen go unemployed. What our fishermen do manage to catch is often declared unfit to eat.

With your support, we can change all this. We must demand an end to toxic dumping in our bay. We must insist that our fishing industry be represented in our State Assembly.

I have been a fisherman for twenty-five years. I know our bay like the back of my hand. I want to work to preserve it for our children, grandchildren, and all future generations.

You know where I stand on the issues. You heard me speak out consistently for clean water standards in my four years on the city council and my two years as your mayor.

Now I want to speak for us in our State Assembly. Won't you help by being a sponsor for the campaign?

Thank you for your support. Together we can clean up our bay.

Sincerely yours,

Len Seashore

* * * * *
(cut here and return the form below)

Yes, I support Len Seashore's Campaign for State Assembly. Enclosed is my endorsement card and my contribution:

Circle one: $25, $50, $75, $100, other _____

As a sponsor who is donating $25 or more, I would also like to help out with the kick-off party in the following ways:

Circle: Provide a food; supply a beverage; donate an auction item; other ways: _____ .

Name: _____
Address: _____
Telephone: _____

* * * * *

Along with this initial letter, include a small envelope with your name and address already printed on it to make it as easy as possible for people to slip a check into the envelope and mail it back right away. You should also include an endorsement card for people to fill out and return in the same envelope. A sample of an endorsement card follows.

LEN SEASHORE for State Assembly
ENDORSEMENT CARD

I/we support and endorse Len Seashore for the State
Assembly election of November 5.

SIGNATURE(S): _____

PRINT NAME(S): _____

STREET _____ CITY _____ ZIP _____

PHONE: Day _____ Night _____

Please check as many as you can.

___ You may use my name publicly as a
supporter.

___ I will contribute $ _____.

___ I will telephone my friends and neighbors.

___ I will distribute campaign literature.

___ I will put a sign on my property.

___ I will help with mailings, letters to the editor,
etc.

___ I have special skills: _____

Please return this card to:
LEN SEASHORE for State Assembly, 555 Fishtail
Road, Lobstercove, MA

Another common way of finding sponsors is simply to call
people and ask them to be sponsors. It is certainly a faster,
cheaper, and more personal way than a letter, and people will
rarely refuse you over the telephone. If you know thirty to fifty
people who are likely to support your candidacy, then just give
them a jingle to explain that you are running for office. State
what you stand for and what you hope to accomplish.

If you have been an activist, most people whom you telephone will already know what you stand for. So you can be
brief. Tell them how much money a sponsor contributes. After
they agree to donate this amount, mention that sponsors generally help out with the kick-off party by providing a platter of
food and an auction item. Would they agree to that, too? Most
sponsors will gladly agree to help out with the kick-off party.
But if they would rather not, don't push it. Graciously thank
them for their donation and sponsorship.

Immediately after your telephone calls, follow up with a letter thanking your sponsors for their promised contributions. This thank you note may be handwritten or typed, but always make it personal. These sponsors will be the backbone of your entire campaign. Include a self-addressed envelope and endorsement card with your brief thank you letter. Following is a sample thank you letter:

Dear Tom and Ellen:

Thank you for becoming sponsors for my campaign kick-off party. The kick-off party will take place at the Shells' home on August 15th. We will be in contact with you to arrange what food to bring. Someone will call to pick up your auction item at your convenience.

Enclosed is a self-addressed envelope for your contribution of $50. Please make out the check to Len Seashore for State Assembly Campaign. I'd be grateful if you'd fill out the endorsement card and return it with the check.

Thanks again for your support. It means a lot to me. Together we can make our community a wonderful place to live.

Yours in friendship,

Len

Making Use of Sponsors' Names

You will be saving a list of all your supporters (people whose names you have collected on endorsement cards). This list will grow dramatically over the months of your campaign. The supporters list will be used repeatedly in newspaper ads and mailers to show your community how many people and what kind of people endorse you.

Of course, a long list of names impresses the undecided voter. But more than sheer numbers, when voters read the list of names, they inevitably search for people whom they know. They think, "Well, if Harry and June are supporting this candidate, he must be okay."

You begin using this list of names to impress people and to create a "join the bandwagon" effect with your invitation to the kick-off party. Following is a sample kick-off party invitation:

CELEBRATION TO KICK OFF LEN SEASHORE'S
CAMPAIGN FOR STATE ASSEMBLY

August 15
Noon to 4:00 P.M.

Contribution: $35 per person, $60 for two

At the home of C. Shell, 12 Clam Court in Lobstercove

* * * * *
(cut here)

Please detach this form and return it to Len Seashore for State Assembly, 555 Fishtail Road, Lobstercove.

☐ YES! I will be there. Here is my contribution of
$ _____ .

☐ Sorry! I can't be there. But here is my contribution
of $ _____ .

Name _____
Address _____
City _____ Zip _____
Day telephone # _____
Evening telephone # _____

* * * * *

Press Releases

You should mail out press releases to local newspapers to publicize campaign events. The first press release announces your candidacy. The second press release should notify the newspapers of the kick-off party. Press releases obey certain guidelines, which are outlined in Chapter Ten. In the meantime, here is a sample press release announcing a kick-off. The press release should be written on campaign stationery.

CONTACT:

Bill Bluegrass, Campaign Director
5 Fiddle Road
Soultown, Louisiana
(444) 444-4444

FOR IMMEDIATE RELEASE
AUGUST 10

PRESS RELEASE

CITY COUNCIL CANDIDATE DONNA GREENBELT

ANNOUNCES HER KICK-OFF PARTY

City council candidate Donna Greenbelt invites you to her kick-off party. The party will take place Sunday, August from 1:00 to 4:00 P.M. at the home of Drake and Henny Eaglenest at 999 Highrock Road. The garden party will feature a gourmet Cajun buffet, wine tasting, entertainment, and an auction.

The price is $25 per person.

"It's time that our city council start representing the people of our city," insists Donna Greenbelt. "We've suffered through years of special-interest groups determining the fate of our town. I believe in government for the people, by the people."

Greenbelt's campaign draws attention to the impacts of oil drilling on every aspect of our lives, from the destruction of our bayous and wildlife to the poisoning of our rivers and land.

Donna Greenbelt is adamant: "The health and welfare of our citizens are at stake. I acknowledge that the oil industry is the economic backbone of our city, but we must begin to show concern for our environment before it is too late."

Greenbelt wants a strictly grassroots campaign. "Everyone in town is welcome to join me in our fight to improve the quality of life in our city."

Kick-off Party Essentials

Location.   The location of your kick-off party will depend on the style of your community. If you live in a rural area, then an outdoor barbecue at a friend's ranch or farm is a natural choice. If you live in the suburbs, a friend's backyard will do nicely.

If you live in a city among apartment and condominium dwellers, then hunt for someone with a spacious apartment. Even better, you might find a supporter among restaurant or cafe owners who is willing to donate the use of his establishment on the day that his restaurant is normally closed.

In any case, try to find a location that will cost you no money! Remember, the essential is that every penny from the kick-off goes to your campaign coffers.

Food committee.   Select a volunteer to chair the food committee. This person is responsible for telephoning sponsors to coordinate what food items each will provide so that you offer a well-balanced buffet. For example, you do not need ten different people bringing deviled eggs.

Your food committee will decide with you whether to serve a full buffet meal or just finger foods, such as hors d'oeuvres and desserts. Or how about a barbecue with a wide variety of salads? Whatever the kind of food, make it good and plentiful. After all, you want your supporters to eat well and have a good time.

Drinks.   You need sponsors to donate wine, beer, and soda. If you live in a community that does not tolerate alcohol, then by all means don't serve it. But if alcohol is an approved social beverage in your town, then serve it. A glass of wine helps your guests relax and enjoy themselves. Most importantly for your campaign coffers, a little wine helps people loosen up for the auction. Whether you serve alcohol or not, make the party fun.

The auction.   It is important to keep in mind that your kick-off is a fundraiser. You have already collected contributions from your sponsors, plus money from your guests, who may have paid $25 or more per person to attend. In addition, a well-run auction may earn thousands of dollars for your campaign.

One or more volunteers are needed to organize the auction to accomplish the following tasks: telephoning sponsors to request auction items; picking up the auction items from the sponsors; typing up a numbered list of the auction items; and presenting the list of auction items to guests as they enter the kick-off party.

At the party itself, the auction items should be on display and numbered in the order of the list itself. Guests will examine the list and the items as they enter the party and often will decide early what items they want to bid on. In order to acknowledge your supporters' generosity, place the donors' names by the auction items on the list.

Your auctioneer should be outgoing and entertaining. A loud, booming voice helps too. Perhaps you know someone in your community with experience as an auctioneer. Sometimes it adds spice to have a team of two people as auctioneers. That way they can play off one another's sense of humor as they present the items. Make your auction as entertaining as it is lucrative.

Following is a sample list of auction items.

KICK-OFF PARTY AUCTION ITEMS

1. $30 gift certificate from Henderson's Hardware Store . . . Value: $30
2. Earrings from Julie's Jewelry Boutique . . . Value: $40
3. Gourmet dinner for four at Joe and Susan's home . . . Value: Priceless.
4. Weekend at the Smiths' lakeside mountain cabin . . . Value: $250
5. Computer table . . . Value: $300
6. Romantic dinner for two at Seaside Lodge . . . Value: $75
7. Louie's famous homemade fudge . . . Value: $20
8. Hot-air balloon ride over the valley. Champagne lunch included . . . Value: $200

9. T-shirts from last four political campaigns . . .
   Value: Priceless.
10. Autographed copy of the novel *League of Liars*, a
    political thriller, by Maritza Pick . . . Value: Priceless
11. Two days of landscaping by Henry . . . Value: $250
12. One day of housecleaning by Alice . . . Value: $100
13. Three bottles of champagne . . . Value: $40
14. Four evenings of babysitting by Sally . . . Value: $125
15. Manicure at Old Town Beauty Shop . . . Value: $20
16. $30 gift certificate from Greenbay Flower Shop . . .
    Value: $30
17. Giant-size teddy bear . . . Value: $45
18. Basket of fruits and vegetables fresh-picked from
    Joan's garden . . . Value: $20

19. Five jars of homemade preserves by Shirley . . .
    Value: $25
20. One day of house painting by Sam . . . Value: $350
21. Environmental attorney Leslie S. offers two hours of
    legal advice . . . Value: Priceless
22. Night at the theater for two to see the play of your
    choice . . . Value: $90
23. Sunday fishing trip on Bob and Liz's boat . . .
    Value: Priceless
24. Family ski weekend . . . Value: $400
25. Backpack . . . Value: $80
26. Tent and camping gear . . . Value: $200
27. Year's membership to four environmental
    organizations of your choice . . . Value: $150
28. One month of lawn-mowing by Judy's son Tommy . . .
    Value: Priceless
29. $50 gift certificate from 101 Flavors Ice Cream Parlor
    . . . Value: $50
30. Year's membership to City Health Club . . . Value: $300

As you can see, successful auctions need only a little bit of imagination. Your supporters are people with a variety of skills to offer. A few supporters may own cabins in the mountains or at the beach to donate for a weekend. Some are undoubtedly good cooks. Many have items hanging around the house that they have meant to get rid of for years. Homemade products are usually well appreciated. In addition, your community is loaded with services and business gift certificates that your sponsors can provide.

A good auctioneer will usually fetch more than the listed value for most items. Aim for a minimum of forty to fifty items for the auction if you expect forty to fifty guests. And be sure that auction items are in a variety of price ranges so that everyone can join the fun and afford to bid on at least one item.

Entertainment.   Many successful kick-offs have no official entertainment. The food, conversation, speeches, and auction provide plenty of entertainment. However, you may happen to know some gifted musicians or singers who are willing to donate their talents. Good music livens up a party and enhances the mood before the speakers take the podium.

For lack of live musicians, tapes or CDs may be played as background music to create a pleasant mood.

Speeches.   The candidate should be introduced with lavish praise by one or more respected citizens of the community. For example, if your mayor endorses you, ask her to introduce you. One soft-spoken city council candidate, who was not used to the spotlight, had the mayor, a city councilman, and the county supervisor introduce him at his kick-off. The endorsements and high praise of the community's leaders lent instant credibility to the candidate's campaign, even though the candidate was by nature a modest, self-effacing fellow.

By some quirk of nature, *Homo sapiens* who are drawn to political office tend to be long-winded. But the kick-off is no place for harangues or lectures. Keep all speeches short and lively.

Microphone and podium.   Always have a microphone and podium. Test the microphone before guests arrive to set it at the proper volume. Guests should not have to strain to hear what the speakers are saying.

Welcome table with buttons and signs.   At the entrance to the kick-off party, place a welcome table with campaign buttons, bumperstickers, and signs. Offer these items to everyone as they enter and leave the party.

At the welcome table, ask everyone who arrives at the party to fill out an endorsement card immediately if they have not already mailed one in. Ask guests to sign the sign-in sheet, requesting name, address, and telephone number. Also supply each guest with a name tag.

Congratulations! By throwing a great kick-off party, you are successfully gathering supporters, campaign workers, newspaper coverage, and thousands of dollars for your campaign treasury. You are on the road to victory!

The Campaign Treasurer

Who should handle the campaign treasury? You, the candidate, may wish to handle all the campaign funds. In fact, this is often the case in grassroots campaigns. But if you have a trusted acquaintance with accounting experience, then by all means take advantage of it and ask her to be the campaign treasurer. The advantage of a treasurer is that it frees the candidate to devote more time to other aspects of the campaign.

The bookkeeping for a political campaign must be scrupulously perfect. There is no room for error. Bookkeeping mistakes—even small ones, even unintentional ones—can cost you the election.

You must know the laws! The government will be checking your books. Campaign financial records are public documents and may be examined by a variety of government agencies. You definitely do not want any trouble with the government over your bookkeeping, so find out every single rule and regulation regarding campaign finances in your city, county, and state.

Contact your state capital's Fair Political Practices Commission (or its equivalent) for a complete guide to "campaign disclosure." These regulations change constantly and are getting more complicated all the time. So be certain to have the most recent regulations at your fingertips. One city clerk told me, "I used to copy a couple pages from the state's campaign disclosure manual to give to each city council candidate. But now the rules are so complex, I don't dare leave out a single one. I recommend that every candidate read the entire manual."

But don't be frightened by the regulations. Although they may be numerous, they are generally straightforward. The state manual on campaign disclosure is a helpful guide on how to set up bookkeeping for a campaign. If you have never run a campaign before, this manual will tell you nearly everything you need to know about campaign bookkeeping and financial disclosure.

After reading your state's manual, if you still have questions, contact your state capital bureau or commission that prepared the manual. Feel free to ask questions until every regulation is clear to you.

Your opposition is going to scrutinize your books. By law, at designated times during the campaign, you must make public your campaign's financial records. Your opposition will go over your financial records with a fine-toothed comb, searching for some point on which to skewer you. If your financial records are in proper order, then you have nothing to worry about.

Conversely, don't miss a chance to examine your opposition's books. Make photocopies of your opponents' list of contributors. Who gave and how much? If you can tell something about a person by the company he keeps, then you can definitely tell a politician by his contributors.

Your opposition's contributors list is an invaluable campaign weapon. For example, it can help you expose the charade of "green advertising," which is brilliantly used to baffle and deceive the public. In television and magazine ads, oil and chemical companies portray themselves as the environmental heroes of the world. Or a beautiful print ad shows eagles in flight over magnificent, rugged canyons. Only after a few seconds of gazing at the eagles does one realize that one is admiring an ad for cigarettes.

Many politicians use this green advertising ploy. They may not support any environmental issues whatsoever, but they say what they think the public wants to hear. You may run against a candidate who is portraying himself as green as a leprechaun. But if you print a list of his contributors—in your mailers, ads, and letters to the editor—that includes all the anti-environmental forces in your community, then you've revealed his true colors to the public.

Other Fundraising Activities

If you are lucky, your kick-off party may well garner most of the money necessary to pay for your entire campaign. But if your campaign or environmental organization requires more funds to cover its expenses, then the following suggestions provide popular methods of fundraising.

Fundraising Through Mailers

The fundraising letter is a common way for candidates and environmental organizations to collect money from supporters. Your supporters share your values, so your appeal can be direct.

You have a few seconds to grab donors' attention once they open the envelope. The first paragraph should pique the reader's curiosity immediately. In her *Fund Appeal Handbook*, Susan LeFever, a Sierra Club expert on fundraising, recommends that the critical first paragraph tell a story, ask a question, assert a surprising statement, or make an immediate appeal for the reader's help. For example, you may begin by boasting of your greatest victory or by alarming readers with the details of an imminent environmental threat.

The closing paragraph is equally important. Tell the reader how much money you need and what you will do with it. Make your request for a $25, $35, $50, or $100 contribution. Stress the urgency of acting quickly and mailing in the donation that very day!

In the body of the letter, list your accomplishments. Focus on specific problems and goals. Offer solutions and hope. Make the supporters feel that their contributions will make a big difference.

Enclose a response form to be returned with the check. This response form may be your endorsement card or a separate card.

On the response card, repeat the thrust of the letter. Following is a sample response card.

Yes, I am happy to support your campaign! You are working to preserve our treasured environmental values. I share your commitment.

Enclosed is my contribution of $25, $35, $50, $100 or other.

Name: _____

Address: _____

Telephone: _____

Mail to: Chris Candidate, P.O. Box 123, Hometown, Pennsylvania

Enclose a small, self-addressed, unstamped reply envelope for the check.

Send a thank you note to all contributors. This simple thank you makes supporters feel appreciated, which smoothes the way for them to donate again in the future.

For further suggestions on how to create a successful fundraising letter, see the mailer section in Chapter Eleven.

Fundraising by Volunteer Telephone Banks

Telephone banks enhance the response to fundraising letters. Volunteers may telephone supporters just before or just after the arrival of the fundraising letter to reinforce its message. Environmental organizations report that telephone banks can increase donations by as much as 30 percent.

It is best to call people from 6:00 P.M. to 9:00 P.M., Monday through Thursday, when you are likely to find them home.

Some volunteers prefer calling from their own homes. However, many telephone bank volunteers enjoy the camaraderie of making calls from the same location, such as a business office with several telephone lines. Set a festive mood. Serve snacks and beverages. Encourage a sense of fun and good humor.

Provide each telephone bank volunteer with a written script. Keep the script brief. Rehearse the script aloud to assure that it is easy to say.

Following is a sample script:

"Hello, my name is Glenda Goodperson. I'm a volunteer for Len Seashore's campaign to represent us in our State Assembly.

We recently sent you a letter about Len Seashore's important accomplishments for our community. Did you receive that letter?

Yes! Wonderful! Then you are aware of his many accomplishments last year as our mayor. And you know how much we need him speaking for us in the State Assembly.

(Insert details of past achievements and future challenges.)

To win the election, we need to raise $7000. Can we count on you to donate $40? No? How about $30? No? Any amount you can give will make a big difference to the campaign. How much would you like to donate?"

If the person declines to contribute money, remain sweet as honey, thank him for his time and past support, and wish him a good evening.

If people do want to pledge money, then ask them to insert a check into the reply envelope enclosed with the fundraising letter. In addition, you may want to send reminder cards. Telephone bank volunteers can fill out and sign preprinted reminder cards and outside envelopes. Mail these reminder cards to people who have pledged by telephone to donate money. For example, during a campaign, a reminder card might read as follows:

Dear _____ ,

Thank you for your pledge of $ _____ to Len Seashore's campaign for the State Assembly.

With your support, Len Seashore can win the election and continue his work for a clean bay in order to revive our struggling fishing industry. We all know that the welfare of our environment and our economy go hand in hand.

Please send your donation in the enclosed envelope. Your generous contribution is more important than ever to the future of our community.

Sincerely,

(Volunteer's Signature)

Accurate records are a necessity. Every volunteer should keep precise notes on people called and the amount each person pledged to donate. Also note whether there was no answer (NA) or the line was busy (B). These accurate records make it easy for future telephone bank volunteers to work from the list of names.

After every telephone bank session, organizers should offer profuse thanks to all telephone bank volunteers. They deserve it.

Coffees

Host a coffee and cake or wine and cheese party in a supporter's home. Invite many people. Charge no admission. At the party, present a brief talk about your environmental organization or election campaign. Ask guests to consider a donation of $25, $50, or more. Pass out envelopes and ask people to donate money then and there. The host or hostess can state how much he or she has already given, to set a standard.

Birthday Fundraisers

A creative fundraising idea is to invite people to your birthday party and request that, instead of gifts, they offer money to your environmental organization or election campaign.

Outings Fundraisers

Lead an architectural tour, a nature walk, an historical tour, a horseback ride, and other outdoor outing events. Charge $10 to $25 per person. Advertise in the newspaper to attract new people to your organization or campaign.

Pyramid Dinners

Pyramid dinners worked successfully to raise funds for the Nuclear Freeze Campaign in California. For example, invite twelve people to dinner at your home and charge $12 per person. Then have two individuals from the original twelve guests invite twelve different people to their own homes, and so on and so forth, for a long chain of delightful dinners. These pyramid dinners are enjoyable and lucrative. A potluck affair with everyone providing a dish makes the dinners simple to organize and easy for the host.

Garage Sales

Someone in your organization is bound to be a garage sale buff. Ask that person to help organize a committee to accomplish the various tasks involved in creating a successful garage sale: to solicit goods by newsletter, to telephone supporters for donations, to arrange for pick-up and delivery of items, to assure publicity, to prepare posters and signs, to find storage space and a garage sale location, to price items, to assign responsibility for the money, and to arrange clean-up duties.

Collect as many items as possible and never overprice them. Garage sales are a great way to recycle possessions while making money.

There are a multitude of imaginative ways to raise funds for your environmental organization or campaign. The following are useful books on the subject:

- *Successful Fundraising: A Complete Handbook for Volunteers and Professionals,* by Joan Flanagan. Contemporary Books, 180 North Michigan Avenue, Chicago, IL 60601.

- *Fundraising for Social Change,* by Kim Klein. Chardon Press, P.O. Box 101, Inverness, CA 94937.

- *How to Create and Use Solid Gold Fundraising Letters,* by Arthur Lambert Cone, Jr., Fund-Raising Institute, Box 365, Ambler, PA 19002.

Don't let fundraising overwhelm you. Remember, fundraising is only a means to an end, not the end itself. If you budget your time, you will learn how to spend your time wisely. Fundraising is only a small part of what you must do to win the election. Time, not money, is your most precious commodity.

Budgeting Your Time: How to Organize

Every community has its own time frame concerning when to begin various aspects of the campaign. When should you begin soliciting sponsors? When to schedule your kick-off party? When should your signs appear around town? When should your ads appear in local newspapers? When are the public debates? When are mailers sent out?

Within your campaign committee, invite a few people who are experienced from previous campaigns. At the very outset of your campaign, have these experienced campaigners make out a list of dates when these various aspects of the campaign were done in previous elections in your community. If you begin the campaign too early, too late, or in the wrong order, the voters will perceive that you are inexperienced with your town's protocol and lose confidence in you.

Then, from your experienced campaigners' list, compose a list of your own for your own campaign. This schedule will help you to focus on each aspect of the campaign at the proper moment. Following is a sample list for a two-month period for a city council election set for November.

CANDIDATE'S SCHEDULE

JULY 1–7: Visit city hall to pick up papers to file for city council election. Also pick up all campaign and financial disclosure regulations. Fill out all the proper forms. Mail press release to newspapers announcing my candidacy.

JULY 8—15: Call potential sponsors for kick-off party. Call Alice to ask if we can use her backyard for the kick-off. Visit several typesetters and printers to compare estimates on costs for mailers and ads. Contact environmental organizations for referrals to local mail houses. Also obtain referrals to companies that make signs and bumperstickers. Compare prices.

JULY 16—23: Have typesetter design campaign stationery with campaign letterhead, kick-off party invitations, and endorsement cards. Organize food and auction committees for kick-off.

JULY 24—30: Mail out thank you notes to sponsors. Visit mail house to confirm that they sent kick-off invitations to proper list of people. Make sure that bumperstickers and signs will be ready before the kick-off. Mail press release to newspapers announcing the kick-off.

AUGUST 1—7: Arrange regular meeting times with campaign committee from now until election day. Ask committee if meeting from ten to noon every Saturday morning is acceptable. Attend to final details of the kick-off party. Write and rehearse my kick-off party speech.

AUGUST 8: KICK-OFF PARTY.

AUGUST 9—16: Organize letters-to-the-editor committee. A minimum of four letters a week from now until election day should appear on my behalf in local newspapers. Organize sign committee.

AUGUST 17—24: Focus on opposition. Research their records. Write up fundraising letter showing how dangerous the opposition is.

AUGUST 24—SEPTEMBER 3: Stake the first batch of my signs at key intersections in town the week before Labor Day. Mail fundraising letter. Organize coffees in various neighborhoods to meet the voters. Contact civic organizations to arrange speaking engagements. Contact local radio and television stations to arrange interviews. Mail out press releases to newspapers for each event.

You get the picture. There is so much to do that you simply must be focused and organized. In September and October, you will be scheduling debates, designing newspaper ads, composing more mailers, putting up more signs, going door to door, seeking endorsements, staffing shopping centers, and speaking to any organization that will agree to listen. The campaign volunteers themselves will be a beehive of activity, helping you every inch of the way.

Remember, good organization is the key to success.

CHAPTER 10

How to Deal Successfully with the Media

How well you deal with the media in your community may determine whether you win the election. This chapter discusses the following aspects of working successfully with the media: press releases, letters to the editor, newspaper advertisements, interviews with newspaper editors and reporters, winning local newspapers' endorsements, radio interviews, and television appearances.

Press Releases

Press releases are short news accounts to be sent out to the news media to announce the events of your campaign—for example, to announce your candidacy, the kick-off party, radio interviews, television appearances, debates with the opposition, coffees given in your honor, your speeches at civic groups and other organizations, outstanding endorsements, etc. You want to keep your name and your issues in the forefront of the public's mind.

The following are basic rules for a good press release:

- Put the source of the release in the upper left-hand corner of the paper. This includes the name, address, and telephone number of the person to contact for more information. The contact person may be the candidate or the campaign director.

- Put the release date, typed in capital letters, slightly below the source information and on the opposite (right-hand) side of the page.

- Sum up the most important information of the press release in the headline in capital letters.

- Use standard 8½-by-11-inch sheets of paper for your releases. Feel free to use your campaign stationery. Use only one side of the paper. Keep the length of the release to one page whenever possible. If you must use more pages, then type "(MORE)" at the bottom of the page. Staple all pages on the top left corner. Underneath the final paragraph of the press release, type "###" or "-30-" or "END" to indicate the conclusion.

- Your release should be typed double-spaced. Leave a three-inch margin on the top of the first page and leave margins on each side that are wide enough for editing.

- Stick to the standard who, what, where, when, and why of journalism.

- Use good-quality paper. White paper is most often used for press releases, but a color other than white may be used to make your press release stand out on an editor's overcrowded desk.

- Don't send news releases that have a copy machine look.

- Find out how far in advance each contact wants your information. For example, a weekly newspaper may require your press release a week or two in advance.

- Don't make the release an advertisement for you. Unconcerned with providing free publicity for a candidate, editors are looking for good stories. So create interesting news for readers. Make the event the crux of the press release. Include quotable quotes from you about the issues.

- The release should be the minimum length necessary to present the facts of interest to the audience.

- Keep your news-release mailing list up-to-date. All editors and reporters like to see releases addressed to them rather than to their predecessors.

The following is a sample press release:

CONTACT:

Cliff Cleanair, Campaign Director
5 Panoramic Way
Breezeville, Georgia
(000) 666-6666

OCTOBER 10
FOR IMMEDIATE RELEASE

ENVIRONMENTAL GROUPS ENDORSE LIZ LEAFBORN

Four environmental groups endorsed Liz Leafborn in her bid for State Assembly. The Conservation Society, the Wildlife League, Citizens for Clean Air, and the Greenbelt Alliance all agree that Dr. Leafborn demonstrates the most environmental concern among the candidates running for State Assembly.

"Dr. Leafborn, as a veterinarian, shows a deep understanding of wildlife concerns," stated the chair of the Conservation Society.

"Liz Leafborn's emphasis on lowering automobile and factory emissions means cleaner air for our state," applauded the president of Citizens for Clean Air.

The Greenbelt Alliance and Wildlife League were impressed by Leafborn's dedication to the creation of new state parks.

All organizations stressed the importance of electing more environmentalists to public office.

To whom do you send press releases? Send them to all your local newspapers, daily and weekly. Address the releases to the newspapers' editors. You may want to send extra releases to newspaper reporters who generally cover election issues or have shown a positive interest in environmental concerns.

Also mail press releases to your local radio and television stations. Address the releases to the appropriate talk show interviewers, newscasters, or producers. Often the producers decide who appears on the shows and what issues are discussed on the air. On local cable shows the producer and host are frequently the same person.

Don't expect the newspapers to print an article about every press release that you mail them. Part of the purpose of the press release is to keep you in newspaper editors' thoughts so that they will think favorably of you when it comes time to decide whom the newspaper will endorse. In addition, editors have their own agendas on how to cover elections. So they may combine several of your press releases into one single story weeks after you mailed them your releases.

If the newspaper neglected to print one of your important news releases, such as the announcement of the date, place, and time of your kick-off party, then contact the newspaper editor immediately. In a cordial manner, remind him that the newspaper overlooked printing an article announcing your kick-off.

Don't make any angry accusations, such as, "I know you support my opposition! You intentionally left my kick-off announcement out of the news!" Never yell at a newspaper editor or reporter. Be polite. A sense of humor always helps too.

For example, you could say to the editor, "I realize that your desk is swamped with news stories. I want to make it as easy for you as possible. How far in advance should I mail you our press releases to make certain that they get in the paper?"

Even if the editor does initially support your opposition, he will appreciate your spirit of understanding and cooperation. Remember, newspaper editors have been known to change their support halfway through a campaign as they learned more about all the candidates. Make it as easy as possible for the editors to know you, like you, and eventually endorse you.

Letters to the Editor

A letter to the editor is a letter mailed to a newspaper commenting on some newsworthy issue or event. You have scanned the letters-to-the-editor page in your local newspapers. You may even be one of the people who reads them avidly. Many people do. Well, now it's time to read those letters carefully. Study their style and length. Note what requirements the various newspapers make on the letters that they print, for you are about to deluge the newspapers with letters of your own.

During a campaign, letters to the editor provide the best method of free advertising for you. Paying for half-page or full-page ads in your local newspapers will be one of the most expensive costs of your entire campaign. But you can obtain months of newspaper coverage absolutely free of charge by an effective letters-to-the-editor campaign.

Letters to the editor permit a discussion of the candidates and the election issues on a regular basis. This allows readers to become familiar with a candidate and what he stands for over a period of months. This public endorsement through letters to the editor gains tremendous credibility for a candidate and is especially important for little-known candidates. In a matter of a few weeks, unknown candidates may become household words through a good letters-to-the-editor campaign.

Letters to the editor prime the voters. After weeks of reading positive views about a candidate in newspaper letters, voters will look favorably on a candidate's official campaign brochures when they are mailed out. Voters will also pay more attention to the candidate's ads. Voters pay special attention to letters to the editor because they are written by neighbors and friends and are not paid political announcements.

Of course, your opposition will not sit idly by and watch your side take possession of the newspapers' editorial pages. They will surely form a letter-writing campaign of their own. An ardent debate is likely to emerge on your newspapers' letters-to-the-editor pages. It is vitally important that your campaign sends more letters to the newspapers than your opposition.

The momentum must be on your side. Newspaper readers often assume that the candidate with the most letters has the most supporters. Furthermore, readers conclude instinctively that if a candidate has so many ardent supporters, there must be a good reason for it. He must be a qualified candidate.

Be aware that letters do more than impress the public—they also impress the newspaper editors. Newspapers generally endorse candidates in every election. If a deluge of letters pours in praising you, open-minded editors will take heed. These letters can strongly influence the editors' choice when it comes time to endorse a candidate.

Your community may be afflicted with a biased newspaper editor who does not personally approve of your candidacy. By the rules of good journalism, the editor must still print letters to the editor and thereby give positive coverage to you. Those letters do a wonderful job of sidestepping any editorial prejudice of the newspapers themselves. Many local newspapers have a policy of printing every letter. Take advantage of those newspapers. Do not bother with newspapers that print only a selective handful of letters.

What form should your letters take? Newspapers generally require that letters to the editor be typed double-spaced. Never handwrite a letter to the editor. Never send in a letter full of spelling and grammatical errors. Stick to the word limit imposed by the newspapers. The shorter your letter, the better the chance of its being printed.

If you have personal stationery, by all means type your letter on that. Otherwise, ordinary white typing paper is most commonly used. Pale-colored shades of paper are fine too, but never use deep reds, purples, or blues, which make it difficult to read the black type on the page.

Sign your full name on the letter. Often newspapers require your address. Some newspapers also request a telephone number, but generally an address will suffice. Date the letter too. Call your local newspapers to find out their specifications.

Your letter-writing committee is essential in a campaign. It's a fact of life that few people feel comfortable writing letters these days. Even some of the most articulate and well-informed people may simply freeze when they see a blank piece of paper in front of them. They may not write a letter at all or may put off writing one until it's too late. That is why this letter-writing committee is so crucial.

At every campaign meeting, you and the campaign director should remind campaign volunteers to write in letters to the editor. But in addition to this reminder, a committee of select letter writers should be formed.

Find out who in your community actually likes to write letters. Ask your campaign volunteers. You probably will not be flooded with offers. Sometimes you may find only one person in your campaign who likes to write letters to the editor. Perhaps you'll be lucky to find six or seven people. Treasure these people. They will form your important letter-writing committee.

This committee will compose letters from ideas supplied by other campaign volunteers who are full of good information and ideas but do not like writing letters themselves. Then these unsigned, typed letters will be passed on to you or the campaign director, who will find individuals to sign these letters.

It is a form of ghostwriting and perfectly legitimate. After all, the people who sign the letters agree completely with the content of the letters. In fact, most people are eager to sign them. They often respond, "That's just what I've been saying. What a good letter! Just how I'd phrase it!"

Everyone who signs a letter written by a campaign letter writer should be told the following:

- Sign your full name and address legibly at the bottom of the letter.

- Date the letter.

- Address the envelope with your return address and the newspaper's address.

- Accept full credit for the letter when your friends and neighbors compliment you on that great letter of yours that just appeared in the newspapers. It is your letter now; you signed it. Enjoy the full credit for it.

Following are some suggestions for your letter writers:

- Print out the letters on a variety of types of paper, using different colors and sizes.

- Print out two or more original copies of the letter so that the same letter may be sent to two or more local newspapers and receive maximum coverage.

- Write letters from a variety of points of view, covering many issues.

- Compose the letters in diverse styles and lengths. But generally keep the letters short.

Never make the letter writers hunt for people to sign the letters. Let the writers focus their energies on the important task of writing itself. The letter writers should pass their letters on to you or the campaign director, who will take charge of getting the letters signed and mailed. Here are some helpful hints for the process:

- After a volunteer has signed all the copies of a letter and addressed the envelopes to the newspapers, then the campaign director should take charge of affixing the postage and mailing the letters. Never let a letter signer take charge of doing the mailing. Too often, letters have an uncanny way of getting lost or delayed.

- If a letter signer approves of the letter but would like to make a few alterations, try to make the changes on the spot with a little white-out, or retype the letter then and there. If you let the person take the letter home, it is likely to lie forgotten at the bottom of some drawer.

- Don't worry the letter writers with revisions. It demoralizes them. They have already put a lot of thought and care into writing and typing the original versions of the letters. So you or the campaign director should retype the letters if occasionally that needs to be done to satisfy a letter signer.

- Use a variety of envelopes and stamps.

- Mail copies of the same letter to every local newspaper. Printed in two or three newspapers, each letter can double or triple its readership.

- Every letter mailed to newspapers must look like an original. Newspapers will not print letters that appear to be photocopies.

- Most newspapers will not continue printing letters signed by the same individuals. Use a variety of supporters to sign the letters.

Letter-writing committees are becoming common even in small-town campaigns, but there is no point in boasting about yours. You may have some truly talented letter writers churning out dozens of terrific letters. It may be tempting to brag about them. But don't! Thank your writers privately. Let the world at large give credit to those who signed the letters. This is part of the magic of putting together a successful campaign.

Newspaper Advertisements

To create your newspaper advertisements, it is essential to have the advice of people experienced in previous political campaigns in your community. Study the ads of past election winners. You may find back issues of newspapers at your local library or at newspaper offices themselves. Note the following:

- What do successful campaign ads in your community look like?

- What size are the ads? Full-page? Half-page?

- Are there photographs of the candidate? How large are the photographs? What is the candidate doing in the photograph? Is there more than one photograph in the ad?

- How large is the type?

- How readable is the text?

- What campaign issues are brought up?

- How many controversial issues are listed?

- Do the ads provide a list of supporters?

- How many supporters are listed?

- In what type size are the supporters' names listed?

The winners of previous elections in your community have a lot to teach you. Study their techniques. Every community has its own style. Feel free to be creative with your ads, yet base your creativity on what has already succeeded in your town. For example, a slick campaign ad that might grab voters' attention in New York City is likely to be completely inappropriate in a Wyoming ranching community.

How many ads should you run? The number will depend on how much money you have in your campaign coffers. Often, grassroots candidates put most of their money into mailing promotional letters to voters. Whatever is left over toward the end of the campaign determines how many ads the candidate may run in the newspapers. There may be only enough money left for one full-page or half-page ad in your local paper to appear the week of the election.

Don't panic if you have only enough money for one ad. If your mailers have been numerous and well done, if precinct walkers have gone door to door, if shopping-center staffers have passed out lots of brochures, if your telephone committee has reminded all your supporters to vote, then voters have heard plenty about you and will remember your name come election day.

When should you place the ads? If you are running only one ad, then place the ad to appear the weekend just before election day. If you have enough money for two ads, then place the second ad at an earlier date or in an additional local paper. Ask your local newspaper what editions have the largest readership. For example, if the weekend edition attracts the most readers, then be sure to place your ad in the weekend edition.

You also must determine which newspaper is most widely read and has the most credibility in your community. You want your ad to get your money's worth of attention. Once again, the advice of experienced campaigners in your community is invaluable in assessing which newspapers should carry your ads.

It is also helpful to study the ads of candidates who lost past elections. What is wrong with their ads? What should you avoid doing in your own ads?

What should your ad contain? At the minimum, you should include the following:

- A flattering photograph of you. Provide the newspaper with a professionally taken black-and-white glossy photograph. Don't rely on photos taken by the newspaper; these can be notoriously unflattering.

- A short list of the most important issues in your town and your stance on them. Be succinct and enumerate only the highest priority issues. Otherwise you will overwhelm the voters with data and leave them confused as to what you truly feel is of greatest importance.

- A brief statement of your qualifications for the job.

- A long list of your supporters. Give special attention to endorsements by newspapers, clubs, organizations, officeholders, and important citizens in your town. People reading the ad will automatically search for friends' and neighbors' names on the list. Uninformed voters who make up their minds at the last moment will read the supporters list and think, "Holy cow! If the Rural Preservation Trust, the Parks Commissioners, and our neighbors Ed and Louise support this candidate, then she must be okay!"

Be sure to make your ad readable. If it is not visually appealing and readable, then you have wasted your money. The type size should be large enough so that people can easily read the text. The names of supporters may be printed at the bottom of the ad in a smaller type size.

Remember, the newspaper ad is just one of the last trumpet calls to voters before the election. Grassroots campaigns rarely have enough money to pay for numerous ads, so prepare one or two outstanding full-page or half-page ads. But put the thrust of your campaign in the area where grassroots campaigns excel: people power. That means letters to the editor, signs, mailers, shopping-center staffers, precinct walkers, and telephone committees to remind people to vote.

Interviews with Newspaper Editors and Reporters

Always be polite with newspeople. If you are rude, abrupt, or insulting, you can count on your attitude being remembered and resented for years to come.

One environmental candidate for city council once told me, "I've got to go for my first interview with the newspaper editor today. I'm not looking forward to it. I view the press as the enemy. They're sure to misquote me to make me look like a fool. I know they're siding with the big business forces in town." It's fair to say that the candidate went to the interview with a bad attitude. At the interview, he verbally attacked the newspaper editor, accusing him of collusion with the big money in town. As you can imagine, this candidate did not favorably impress the editor, who printed a scathing article about him along with a photograph that made him look oddly like a pig.

Nonetheless, this same editor soon realized that the majority of his newspaper's readers were in favor of more environmental awareness. Perceiving this change in tide among his readers, he allowed the newspaper to endorse other ecology-minded candidates for the city council seats. However, the abusive candidate was left out in the cold.

If you have an interview with an editor or reporter who is antagonistic, try using humor as a weapon. A good sense of irony goes a long way to charm your opposition and to diffuse difficult political situations. Humor, irony, and cordiality will score points with everyone—even your adversaries.

It is said that politics makes strange bedfellows. How true!

Like the above-mentioned newspaper editor, many people change their opinions over time. Someone who is your arch-enemy today may be your principal supporter a few months from now, once he sees the light. So never insult anyone personally. Always make it as easy as possible for people to come over to your side. In addition, people may disagree with you on today's controversial issue but be in complete agreement with you regarding next year's hot controversy. You may find yourself working hand in hand with someone at whom you were shaking your fist only last year.

Is the press the enemy? By my emphasis on cordiality and self-control in dealing with the press, you can tell that many environmentalists have been riled by interviewers. But the press is not the enemy. Far from it. The press provides free coverage for your cause through its editorial pages and its articles. The more a community shows its concern for environmental issues and candidates, the more the local press will cover these concerns. Good local press is a reflection of the community, not its enemy.

Following are a few tips in how to deal with editors and reporters.

- Mail press releases regularly to keep editors and reporters informed of your activities.

- Get to know a newspaper's editor and your favorite reporter personally. Call to ask for an appointment or invite them out for coffee. Let them get to know you and like you.

- Provide useful, factual information for various story ideas.

- Show an interest in their problems and concerns. How may you help them? Find out what they believe are the most important issues in your community. What do they personally care most about?

- If a reporter writes a good article about your cause, call to thank him.

- If a reporter writes an inaccurate article about your cause or misquotes you, call him and politely suggest corrections to his article. If the errors in the article are serious, you can always write a letter to the editor pointing out the inaccuracies. You may also ask the reporter to write a follow-up article with a more accurate depiction.

- Remember, even if a newspaper's editor and reporters are not on your side when the campaign begins, they may change to your side by election day. So always treat them with respect and courtesy as potential allies.

Newspaper Endorsements

Congratulations! Your local press endorsed you! Most newspapers, large and small, will endorse candidates shortly before the election after having observed the various campaigns and interviewed the candidates. Let's say you won your community newspaper's endorsement.

The newspaper will print an editorial explaining why it endorsed you. If this editorial is particularly well written, then reprint it (with permission from the newspaper) and make it part of your final mailing to voters. If time permits, print lots of extra copies of the editorial. Have your precinct walkers and shopping-center staffers pass out the copies along with your other campaign brochures. Also mention the endorsement in your newspaper ads.

If the endorsement comes at the last minute, then you can print up a postcard boasting of the endorsement and quoting the best lines from the editorial as a last-minute mailer to voters.

Although newspaper endorsements help greatly, many grassroots candidates win elections without a newspaper's endorsement. So don't despair if your local newspapers disappoint you. If you have strong grassroots support, you can still win. Remember, if you have run a strong letters-to-the-editor campaign, voters have already read lots of rave reviews about your cause in the newspapers.

Radio Interviews

First, call all of your local radio stations to find out who are the talk show hosts and their producers. It is usually the producer who arranges the guests and schedules the interviews. However, often the interviewer and the producer are the same person, particularly on smaller radio stations.

Next, mail press releases to radio interviewers and their shows' producers. This gives them a chance to read about you. Then follow up the press release with a telephone call. Introduce yourself not only as a candidate but as an expert on the crucial issues in your community.

What will the talk shows be looking for? Their hosts are looking for controversial topics and experts on those controversies. They want dynamic, informative guests who stimulate their radio listeners. They are not generally interested in promoting your candidacy. They definitely are not interested in hearing you brag about your achievements for an hour.

In order to be invited to appear on a radio interview program, don't focus on your publicity needs. Rather, think: "What does the radio show need? What are the key issues in my community?" Suggest to the host and producer a show on the hottest controversies in your community. Portray yourself as an expert on those issues and volunteer to appear as a guest to discuss them.

You may wish to have your campaign director or another friend make the initial telephone calls to the radio stations to schedule the interviews. Since most people feel awkward boasting about themselves, it is easier for someone else to rave about your expertise, wit, and sundry other qualities. Also, radio producers are accustomed to dealing with agents or publicists to arrange interviews.

If you want the interview to cover specific areas on which you truly are an expert, then give the interviewer a list of questions to ask you. The interviewer will usually be grateful for the help since he may know little about you or the issues you plan to talk about. By providing a list of prepared questions, not only do your rehearsed replies seem impressive, but you also help

the interviewer appear knowledgeable to the listeners. A fumbling interviewer makes you look bad too.

Prepare in advance some humorous and some poignant anecdotes to illustrate the points that you plan to make during the interview. The interview may appear spontaneous to listeners, but the better prepared you are in advance, the more successful the interview will be.

Finally, expect no pay. Radio stations generally do not pay their guests. Your payment is the fact that hundreds or thousands of listeners have heard your name and your ideas. It's a fantastic advertisement for your cause. That is payment enough.

Television Appearances

In national and statewide elections television now plays a major role. At national and state levels, television's influence works against grassroots movements and against any serious debate of real issues. Television has reduced political campaigns to sound bites, snazzy campaign slogans, and photogenic candidates.

Television ads are extremely expensive, so candidates are forced to spend much of their time fundraising millions of dollars to be funneled into public relations firms, ad agencies, and commercial television ad slots. As a rule, grassroots campaigns have less money to spend on such extravagantly expensive television advertising and are therefore often completely left out of the television viewers' perception of election choices.

This is a major flaw in the role of television in American elections. In many other countries, equal television time is assured all candidates. They do not need to pay for it. However, in the present American system, the political side with more money obtains more television attention. If a political candidate or cause does not have millions of dollars to spend for television ads, then they get no coverage. Not very democratic. But so it goes.

On the national and state scene, television's role as a major form of entertainment also lessens candidates' ability to discuss the hard facts. A candidate who claims that the economy is rosy and promises no new taxes is likely to get smiles from weary television viewers. Meanwhile, a realistic candidate who wants to discuss the national debt, environmental destruction, the homeless problem, rising unemployment, declining education, and the painful recession is likely to be viewed as too depressing. Viewers may change the channel. Candidates know that they are competing with cheery situation comedies.

It is a pity that television advertising has invaded elections in major cities so that big-city candidates are held hostage to the superficiality and high cost of television ads. The reason that grassroots campaigns can be so influential at local levels is because television plays little or no role. Other than in major cities, television's role in local elections is minor. Newspapers remain the main medium of election coverage in local elections.

Outside of major cities, local television stations are also more accessible. They offer interview and public affairs programs on local concerns on which candidates may appear at no cost.

Because local elections are free of television's sound-bite bondage, the real issues may be debated in depth. It is a strange irony that a local parks bond issue may receive more incisive analysis in a local newspaper than the national environmental policy does on the national news. That is why there is still so much power at the local level.

The procedure for getting booked on local television interview programs is the same as for radio. The only difference is that there is more competition to appear on television programs, so your campaign manager will have to push harder, make more telephone calls, and mail out more press releases to get you on the tube. Be persistent. As with radio, television interviewers and producers are more likely to schedule you if you present yourself as an expert on vital controversies, not just another candidate wanting attention.

Don't overlook local cable networks. They offer a rich variety of community-oriented programs. Brainstorm how you can fit into their formats for an appearance.

Televised debates offer you another forum. Local television stations often sponsor debates for candidates. However, if your local station isn't willing to organize a debate, then have a community group, such as the League of Women Voters, organize one. Invite the television station to cover it, stressing the enormous community interest in the issues to be debated. When talking with the station manager or producer, feel free to wax eloquently patriotic, accentuating community-based television's duty to inform viewers about the candidates and issues.

Following are some tips for good debating:

• Always stay in control of your emotions. Never get angry or yell.

- Be prepared for attacks from your opposition.

- Never make wild accusations. Be factual. Use your opposition's past record, actions, and words to show what he truly stands for.

- Define the campaign issues in your terms.

- Never let yourself be put on the defensive. Listeners perceive defensiveness as weakness.

- Fill the audience with your supporters, to applaud vigorously at the right times and to ask the right questions to make you look good. Audience response can set the tone of the entire debate.

Some final advice on proper dress for television: Solid colors photograph best; television cameras make busy patterns look fuzzy. Also, a little makeup, such as powder on your face, can stop the bright lights from giving your nose and forehead too much shine.

In summary, the print, radio, and television media provide your cause with tremendous opportunities for coverage. Respect the media. Use them well and they will serve you well.

CHAPTER 11

Mailers, Signs, Bumperstickers, and Absentee Ballots

E very successful grassroots campaign needs good mailers, signs, and bumperstickers. Also, absentee ballots sometimes play a key role in campaign strategy. The following guidelines will help you utilize these important campaign tools effectively.

Mailers

What is a mailer? It is any communication that your campaign mails to the voters. A mailer may be in the form of a letter, an article, a postcard, a brochure, or a newsletter. Many campaigners believe that mailers are the key to winning elections. They inform voters about the candidates and the issues. Your mailings to the community should be carefully thought out and worth their weight in gold.

Start out with an eye-catching envelope. Place a phrase on the envelope that encourages people to open it. This phrase may be funny or alarming, but it should arouse people's curiosity enough to make them want to open the envelope. By the end of a campaign, some voters are tired of campaign literature cluttering up their mailboxes. They toss campaign letters without even opening them. So your envelope itself must tantalize them.

For example, a countywide campaign in favor of a one-cent tax increase in order to buy more public open space put a drawing of a penny on the envelope with the words: "A penny for your thoughts."

Other campaigns have used interesting clip art on envelopes. A campaign to save a forest from a lumber mill used a drawing of lush trees with a large chainsaw looming over them. Sheets and notebooks of clip art are available at art supply stores for a few dollars, and typesetters usually have a good selection of clip art on file.

Another clever device to pique people's curiosity is to put a riddle or question on the envelope that relates to the most controversial issue in your campaign. Voters will tear open the envelope to satisfy their urge to find out the answer to the question. For example, one ecology-minded city council candidate was running against someone who was claiming to be an environmentalist, although the latter's past record indicated an open disdain for environmental concerns. The real nature lover printed on her envelopes the question, "Why does a chameleon change colors?" A clip art drawing of a chameleon appeared beneath the question. Inside, the letter used the theme of the chameleon's camouflage to demonstrate how her opposition was pretending to be an environmentalist to deceive the voters. The catchy riddle and graphics stuck in voters' minds.

The graphics of your mailer will determine whether people read it or not. Here are a few suggestions for creating effective mailers:

- The paper should be of good quality.

- Use color. If you use white paper, then print the campaign's logo or letterhead in your campaign colors. (Your signs, bumperstickers, letterhead, etc., should all be in your same campaign colors.)

- Use clip art.

- The text of the letter should be clearly and neatly typed, with no errors.

- Check art supply stores for border boards, which can frame a letter with appealing, appropriate designs.

- The type size of the text should be readable. Do not reduce type size so that you can cram more words onto a page. Better to keep your letter short and the type size readable.

- Make key points in your letter stand out visually by putting them in bold type or underlining them.

- Use succinct lists of key points introduced by bullets, which are visual devices such as asterisks, dots, or dashes. The text you are now reading exemplifies the use of bullets to make the key points stand out.

- Use an appealing photo of yourself.

- Ask your typesetter and printer for advice on how to make your mailers as visually attractive as possible. Be creative.

To Whom Should You Mail?

Ideally, if your campaign funds permitted, you would send as many mailers as you could to the entire community. However, mailers are costly. So, realistically, you should plan to mail to a select portion of your community.

There is no point mailing your campaign literature to people who never vote. Therefore, frequent voter lists are invaluable. These lists can be purchased from mailing houses that specialize in providing address lists. These mailing houses print the address labels, affix them to the envelopes, and mail the letters for you. Some mailing houses also print and fold letters and stuff them into envelopes. They also may let you use their bulk mailing permit number. Ask various environmental organizations and businesses in your area for recommendations for reliable mailing houses. Also check the telephone directory.

Other kinds of lists are also available: lists of registered voters, of Democrats, of Republicans, of specific neighborhoods, of environmental organization members. If you plan on targeting specific groups, ask your mailing house what variety of lists they offer. They may surprise you! Your local registrar of voters office can also supply you with various lists.

You can obtain a bulk mailing permit from your local post office if your mailing house won't supply one. This permit allows you to mail large quantities of letters for a special reduced postage.

What Should Your Mailer Communicate?

Every mailer should include a hard-hitting attack on your opposition. Make clear what your opposition represents and how that will negatively change the community. Voters must understand exactly what separates you from your opposition. What makes you special? How do you represent the best interests of the voters?

An effective means of revealing what your opposition really believes is to use his own words against him. By placing contradictory quotes side by side, you can reveal your opposition's hypocrisy. It helps if someone in your organization maintains a file on all the outrageous statements your opposition has made. Always list the source of the quote, such as the name and date of the newspaper where the quote appeared. This adds unassailable credibility to your mailer. Following is a sample text from a mailer designed to show that a candidate's words contradict his lofty claims:

As part of his campaign rhetoric, Jon Doe has often proclaimed himself to be an environmentalist. However, let the record speak:

"I am behind the Board of Realtors 100 percent. We need to build, build, build in this town. We can't let any neighborhood sentimentality for a little meadow or a few deer stand in our way of major new developments." Jon Doe addressing the Board of Realtors meeting, *The Voice*, April 11.

Jon Doe's campaign rhetoric claims that he is a friend to all neighborhood concerns. But at a developers' luncheon only a few months ago, Doe stated:

"I support every developer in this county. We need to build up our city's tax base at all costs. We can't afford to pay attention to special-interest groups like the neighborhoods." *The Voice*, January 20, 1992.

A few more quotes like these and you have stripped your opposition of any credibility whatsoever.

In your mailers, your position should be made clear as a bell. After you scare the pants off voters by revealing what your opposition represents, you should outline your position and explain how you will benefit the community. Be succinct. Stick with the facts.

Avoid nice, sweet, forgettable mailers. Politics is not a tea party. Campaign letters with no bite—that is to say, with no solid information as to the issues and the candidates' positions—are a waste of postage. Voters do not want to hear that everything is wonderful and gee, gosh, golly, you are such a terrific candidate. Voters know that the community has problems, and they want elected officials who can identify those problems and who are able to solve them.

Fear and anger are two of the most motivating forces. In politics, they are essential motivators. Indifferent residents become dedicated activists if they fear that their own community, their own family, their own finances, or their own values are threatened.

With environmental concerns, arousing people's fear and anger is easy because there is so much to be angry and frightened about. Take full advantage of this in your campaign mailers. Whether the issues in your community are pollution, toxics, recycling, conservation, traffic congestion, or overdevelopment, always make the voters aware of what is *personally* at stake for them. What do they chance to lose? How are they *directly* impacted by the issues?

If you can make average citizens feel that they have something personally at stake in the election, then they will vote and they will vote for you.

Formats for Mailers

Newspaper format.   The newspaper format is very effective. Design one of your mailers as a four-page newspaper. This is easy and inexpensive. Following are some tips for such a format.

- Print the mailer on newsprint, which not only makes your mailer look like a real newspaper, but also has the advantage of being a less expensive paper.

- Make the newspaper look authentic. People tend to peruse a newspaper even when they toss other campaign literature. Give your newspaper a name and print it as a masthead on the front page, such as "Hometown News," "Voters Times," etc. But make certain that no newspaper in your area already has that same name.

- Print in clear letters at the bottom of the front page exactly who is paying for the mailer. For example, "Paid for by the Committee to Elect Jean Green." In fact, this statement of who is paying for the printed matter should appear on all of your campaign literature by law.

- Use bold headlines.

- Print your text in large, easy-to-read type.

- Use appropriate clip art.

- Use attractive photographs of you.

- If a certain environmental issue is hot news in your campaign, then print a dramatic photograph of the site involved. For example, if your community is opposing a proposed gigantic high-rise complex, show an appealing photograph of the cozy neighborhood that now exists on the site. The headline could read: "Threatened with Destruction!" If you are opposing the damming of a river, print an alluring photograph of the river, next to a bleak photo of a concrete dam.

- All photographs must be top quality. Never use a blurry or second-rate photograph.

- You can print a great deal of information with this newspaper format; you have four large sides of paper to work with. But never overwhelm the voters with data. Focus on a few key issues that the voters care most about.

- Be concise and factual. Do not ramble or harangue.

- The newspaper format lends authority to the text. Try to keep your "articles" in line with newspaper style and appearance.

- The newspaper makes a great handout for your shopping-center staffers and precinct walkers to give to voters.

Postcards.   Postcard mailers have the advantage of being cheaper to print and to mail. They also will be read by virtually everyone who receives them. Postcards are useful for reiterating the key issues, reminding people to vote, and disseminating last-minute information, such as recent endorsements by newspapers and organizations.

Reprints of newspaper pieces.   Perhaps one of your local newspapers endorses your position or printed an excellent editorial supporting your candidacy. You can reprint this (with the newspaper's permission) and use it as a mailer in itself. Be sure to add it to the campaign literature that you pass out at shopping centers.

Hit pieces.   Hit pieces are hard-hitting letters mailed to the community just before election day so that the opposing candidate has no time to respond to the accusations. Hit pieces are often based on innuendo and distortions of the truth. Hit pieces were once regarded as an unethical campaign practice. However, today hit pieces have become common even at the grassroots level, even in small towns. Your side should anticipate a hit piece being targeted against you. This is why your own mailers should include hard-hitting assaults on your opposition's positions, when necessary. But never lower yourself to use lies and innuendo. The truth usually supplies plenty of honest, forthright reasons why you are the best candidate.

Hit pieces are often very simplistic in nature. One particular hit piece targeted a strong environmental candidate running for reelection as mayor. The hit piece was designed to look like a report card. It rated the mayor on various aspects of government and gave him an "F" in every subject. The simplistic graphics greatly influenced the voters. The environmentalist lost the election.

Never underestimate the power of hit pieces. In the above-mentioned election, followers of the environmental mayor were alarmed by the hit piece and urged the campaign organizers to mail out an immediate response to voters and to implement an immediate telephone bank to clarify the true issues to the voters. However, the overly confident campaign leaders responded: "We need not respond to such lowly tactics. The voters are intelligent. They'll know the truth!" Well, the voters did not know the truth. Remember, voters must be told the truth by your campaign. Never let a hit piece go unchallenged.

Hit pieces generally attempt to distract from the real issues by concocting phony issues or trumped-up accusations. Let the voters know that they are being insulted by an explicit attempt to deceive them. But never let negative tactics and charges of foul play color the tone of the election. Voters become dismayed and sometimes do not know whom to believe. So after disclosing the foul play of others, always reiterate the positive aspects of your candidate. End the campaign on a constructive note.

Signs

Campaign signs are used to establish name recognition. Voters should see your name on signs all over town so that when they read letters to the editor, receive campaign mailers, and

see your name on the ballot, they will pay special attention to your side.

Signs have the same impact as advertising billboards. But, in an election, the product that you are trying to make appealing is the candidate. What goes through voters' minds? If voters see lots of signs for you, they assume that lots of people support you. And if lots of people support you, there must be something good about you. So they'll want to learn more about your candidacy.

Signs only have room enough to show your name and the office for which you are running. There is no room on a sign for substance. It's just an attention-grabber to encourage voters to think often of you as a candidate. But campaign signs play a vital role in campaign strategy.

What Should Your Signs Look Like?   Your signs should be simple and readable. There is no need for fancy signs. Your name should appear in large, bold letters taking up most of the sign. In smaller letters, under your name, is room for the office to which you are aspiring. Two sample signs follow:

> # NED NEIGHBOR
> ## City Council

> ## Elect
> # MARCIA MARSH
> ## Mayor

There is no need to clutter your signs with fancy artwork or catchy slogans, which really only distract from the sign's important message: your name and the political office.

If you happen to be inspired by a sensational campaign slogan that you simply cannot resist, then put it on the sign in smaller letters. But never permit a slogan to obscure or diminish your name, which must appear in big, bold letters.

The size of campaign signs varies. Take note of the best signs from previous elections in your town. Model your signs on these. A sign that is approximately two feet long and two feet high is small, but adequate, if the lettering is clear and large.

If your sign is too large, it will be too unwieldy to fit onto a stick. If your sign is too small, no one will notice it. The sign should be able to fit into people's windows. Some ardent supporters like to place these signs in their living room windows and business fronts facing out to the street, where passersby can see them. This is terrific advertising.

Your signs should be in your campaign colors, which should differ from every other candidate's colors. After a while, voters should be able to identify your signs from the colors alone. Select two contrasting colors; this allows the printed letters to stand out. One color is for the background, the other is for the letters. If you choose two colors that are too similar, then the lettering will blend into the background and be hard to read.

Effective contrasting colors are: yellow letters against red background, white letters against dark blue, white letters against dark green background, black letters against bright yellow, deep purple letters against white. You get the idea.

Where to Buy Your Signs?

There are mail order houses throughout the country that specialize in providing promotional materials. At the earliest stage of the election campaign, make queries into these companies. Call them and ask them to mail you their brochures. Shop around for high quality, reliability, and fair prices.

To find these promotion-oriented mail order firms, ask first for recommendations from acquaintances who have run for office before. Contact local environmental organizations, as well as advertising and public relations firms in your area, for their recommendations. Next try the Yellow Pages. You may have an excellent company right in your hometown. Compare prices and quality carefully.

Make sure your signs are made so that they will endure any type of weather, such as wind, rain, and even that freak snowstorm. The signs must be sturdy and treated for protection against water damage.

Make certain that the company takes pride in delivering in a timely fashion. There is no point ordering a couple of hundred signs if they do not arrive until the day before the election.

Many promotion-oriented mail order companies will supply your campaign buttons and bumperstickers too.

When and Where to Put Up Your Signs?   The timing depends on what your community is accustomed to. Find out when the first signs went up in the last election in your town. In many cities, signs go up at least two months before election day. Plan to put up your signs earlier than is customary.

Get your signs up first. Whoever puts up their signs first will receive all the public attention for a week or two. Those weeks of extra name recognition are especially important if you are not already well known in the community. For that week or two, the public sees only your signs. It is a good head start on the campaign.

Before you put up any signs, call your city hall and inquire about local regulations regarding placement of signs. You do not want to break any laws. Communities vary. For example, in some cities, it is unacceptable to attach signs to public poles such as those that support stop signs, bike path signs, direction signs, utility poles, etc. However, we all have visited cities where campaign signs are displayed on every public sign pole available. In some communities, the public would take offense if candidates used the public poles—as if candidates were defacing public property—but other cities do not seem to mind at all. So research what is tolerated and legal in your town.

In every community, there are key places where signs pop up during elections. These places are along major streets, at intersections, and near highway entrances and exits.

Also ask your supporters to place your signs in their homes and businesses. Front yards and windows facing the street are good spots to place signs. Voters traveling around town will be impressed to see lots of your signs on private property. Such a bold display shows committed supporters.

Staking Your Signs

Rather than relying on public poles to supply wood, count on providing your own stakes. Visit your local lumber yard and describe exactly what you need the wooden stakes for. Mention that you will be stapling signs to the stakes, so the stake should have flat sides. One end of the stake should be pointed for insertion into the ground.

Give the lumber yard plenty of advance notice because they may have to special-order or make the stakes for you. Stakes should be approximately three to five feet high. When ordering the length of the stake, keep in mind that six to twelve inches of it will be stuck in the ground.

To attach your signs to the stakes, place two signs back to back around one stake. Your name is thereby visible in two directions. That way, people will be able to read your sign from both directions on the street.

Staple the four corners of the two signs together. If you do not affix the two signs' corners together, the edges will flop around with every little breeze. The corners will droop and eventually reach a sorry state, possibly making the sign unreadable. Staple or nail the middle borders of the signs securely to the stake.

How do you put your signs in the ground? When you're at the lumber yard, ask for a metal stake of the same approximate diameter as your wooden stakes. Hammer the metal stake into the ground to make the hole for the wooden stake, then slide your wooden stake into the hole. Never hammer hard on your wooden stake to make the hole. The wooden stake is likely to shatter or split.

Attach your sign an inch or two below the top of the wooden stake. This extra inch or two at the top of the stake allows you room to tap gently on it with a hammer to insert it into the premade hole—without damaging your sign.

Attaching Your Signs
to Metal and Wooden Poles

If it is acceptable in your city to attach signs to public poles, then take advantage of it. To display signs on metal poles, put your sign on its usual wooden stake and then place the sign and wooden stake against the metal pole. Bind the wooden stake to the metal pole by winding wrapping tape around them both. Use the wrapping tape liberally to secure the sign firmly. To attach your sign to a wooden pole or fence post, nail your sign and wooden stake into the pole or post. When using tall poles, take advantage of their height to place your sign high enough for maximum visibility.

Sign Vigilance

Be prepared to have your signs stolen. It often happens in elections that the opposition will steal or vandalize your signs. You must be prepared for this. The only solution is to put up more signs.

Make a big issue of any theft or vandalism in your letters to the editor. Tell the public how your opponents are thieves or hooligans and how this behavior reflects their disdain for the democratic process. Never retaliate by stealing the opposition's signs. That will only escalate the sign-stealing war. Nothing is gained.

On a weekly basis, patrol the streets to replace signs that were knocked over by the wind or stolen by your opposition. In the last two weeks before the election, patrol the streets more frequently.

Large Signs

In the last few weeks before an election, large signs are often displayed on streets. The easiest way to obtain large signs is to order a bigger version of your existing signs from your mail order company. You only need to order a few of these larger signs since they belong at the most visible, most heavily visited parts of town. They also are frequently used along highways and in open fields.

Remember that the larger the sign, the stronger its backing must be to support it. The mail order company itself may offer the option of incorporating a sturdy backing onto your larger signs.

If you have covered your community thoroughly with smaller signs, then your campaign should question whether it really needs any large signs. They may be superfluous. However, your campaign committee may agree that a few large signs are required for major intersections in town.

In grassroots campaigns, large signs are often homemade. To make a homemade sign, go to the lumber yard for sheets of the desired size of plywood for your sign. In your yard or garage, cover the wood with a light shade of waterproof paint. Let the paint dry. Make a stencil of what lettering you want to appear on the sign, then place the stencil over the wood and paint over the stencil letters with a dark color of waterproof paint. Let this paint dry. Finally, install the large signs with adequate support in the back so that they do not blow over with the first freak storm of the season.

When making signs, don't hesitate to ask for free advice. Your local paint stores and professional sign painters will be happy to answer your questions and give you some helpful advice. Give them a call.

Although grassroots signs may be homemade, they should not look amateurish. They better look good. That means no smeared or runny paint. It is better to have no large signs than poorly made ones. Otherwise, these signs will work against, rather than for, you.

You could also contact professional sign-painting firms to determine the cost of having professionals design and paint your large signs. This can be expensive. But if you have the money to spend, and if you feel these large signs are important to your campaign, then go for it.

As a courtesy to the community, after the election, arrange for supporters to remove all of your signs.

Bumperstickers and Buttons

Generally, only your most ardent supporters will put bumperstickers on their cars and wear buttons. Bumperstickers can be hard to peel off, and buttons can make holes in shirts. Furthermore, many people simply do not like to wear their politics on their sleeves—or on their bumpers and chests.

In hotly contested campaigns, more folks are willing to display their political bias, and you may have to order more bumperstickers and buttons than you expected. But, in general, people are not wild about bumperstickers and buttons; so order only enough from your mail order company for your campaign workers and staunchest supporters. After all, no grassroots campaign can afford to waste money.

How should your bumperstickers and buttons look? The same principles apply to buttons and bumperstickers as apply to signs. Keep the message simple and bold. The candidate's name should be as large as possible, with the political office in smaller, yet readable letters. The bumperstickers and buttons should be in the same campaign colors as your signs.

Your precinct walkers and shopping-center staffers should

definitely wear your campaign buttons to identify themselves as supporters when they hand out campaign literature.

Absentee Ballots

Absentee ballots are forms that allow registered voters to vote early by mail in an election. People vote by absentee ballot for all kinds of reasons. Persons who travel a great deal or who have hectic schedules often prefer the convenience of an absentee ballot because their schedules do not permit them to make it to the polls on election day. Also, people who are bedridden or mobility-impaired appreciate being able to vote from the comfort of their homes.

Absentee ballots have become critically important in big-city and statewide elections. Gubernatorial campaigns, for example, will conduct costly voter surveys and then do target mailings only to their side's supporters, encouraging them to vote by absentee ballot. The absentee ballot response has been credited with winning gubernatorial and big-city elections, especially in close races.

Some election issues, such as school bond measures, may be kept intentionally low-key so as not to arouse any opposition. In these cases, the pro-bond campaign contacts supporters and encourages them to vote by absentee ballot. Other people in town may not realize that this measure is on the ballot or even that an election is going on.

Are absentee ballots important to your campaign? In grass-roots campaigns where a major get-out-the-vote effort succeeds through the telephone bank, precinct walkers, shopping-center staffers, and mailers, absentee ballots may be of little or no importance to your victory. However, if you feel that it is significant to tap absentee voters, then contact your local registrar of voters, from whom you purchase the list of absentee voters. Contact only your supporters on the list.

CHAPTER 12

The Campaign's Essential Volunteers

T he source of strength in a grassroots campaign is people power. Enthusiastic volunteers generously donate their time and energy. These essential volunteers are the heroes and heroines of the democratic process.

Shopping-Center Staffers

Campaign workers who distribute your brochures at shopping centers will remind voters that there is an election going on and that they should vote for you.

Voter apathy is a sad fact of life. In American elections, often less than 50 percent of eligible people vote. This is the lowest voter turnout in any world democracy. For example, in Australia, people are required by law to vote and are fined if they do not. However, until such mandatory voting is required in the United States, voter apathy is a reality to be dealt with. By grassroots methods, this apathy can be transformed into involvement and commitment. Staffing shopping centers is a wonderful way to inform and excite the public about upcoming elections.

Stationing volunteers at shopping centers is truly a grass-roots method of spreading the word. For one thing, the price is

right. It's free. Campaign workers volunteer their time to stand outside a grocery store or post office, pass out campaign literature, and chat with passersby. It provides an invaluable one-on-one dialogue about the issues and candidates.

You will rarely see your well-heeled, well-financed opponents staffing shopping centers. They are busy relying on fancy, slick mailers and expensive ads to attract the voters' attention. As a grassroots campaigner, you are likely to have the shopping centers all to yourself. This is a tremendous asset.

Choose locations where there is maximum foot traffic. The busiest grocery store, drugstore, or post office is often a good spot. If your community has more than one busy shopping center, then have shopping-center staffers at three or four of the most popular places. If you have enough volunteers to staff even more locations, then by all means staff as many popular centers as you can.

Your campaign should begin staffing shopping centers a minimum of three weekends before the election. In most communities, weekends are the busiest times at shopping centers and thus provide the best time to make contact with the maximum number of people. Moreover, people tend to be more relaxed on weekends and more approachable.

Once your campaign committee has decided which stores to target, it is a courtesy to telephone the store manager for permission to set up a small table in front of the store. Tell the manager that the purpose of the table is to encourage people to vote in the upcoming election. He will rarely refuse you permission for such a patriotic cause.

When setting up, place your table a short distance from the main doors so that people leaving and entering the store must see you, but never block the entrance and exit to the store. If possible, set up your table so that cars driving by or parking in the lot will see you too. Tape large campaign signs around all sides of your table to promote your candidate or cause. The words on these signs should be clearly visible from afar. With these signs, even if people do not approach your table, they still see your message.

On top of your table you should have campaign brochures, bumperstickers, signs, anything to pass out to the public. Be prepared to answer questions. Some people may want clarification about certain issues. Make sure that your campaign material will answer all of their questions and hand out your brochures liberally. Hand out more expensive items such as signs and bumperstickers mainly to diehard supporters who you know will put them up. There's no point giving a sign to someone who will dump it in the trash as soon as he returns home.

Caution: It takes only one gust of wind to blow all of your brochures into the nearest puddle in the parking lot. So carry along small paperweights to place on top of your stacks of campaign literature. These little items save you lots of paper-chasing.

How many people should staff a table? Often, two people staff each shopping-center table. The buddy system works well to keep enthusiasm high. It is also useful to have two people present if a sudden crowd forms around the table to ask questions and pick up brochures.

Nonetheless, gregarious volunteers often do fine staffing a table all by themselves. One dynamic woman with whom I once shared a table was a one-woman cheering section. She would greet passersby with a big grin, asking them what they thought about the hot issues in the election campaign. Every passerby loved chatting politics with her. She converted every undecided voter over to our side. She had such a good time staffing shopping centers on weekends that she volunteered to work on Friday evenings staffing a table all by herself. She single-handedly did more to get people to the polls on election day than anyone else in town.

Shopping-center staffers should be friendly at all times. Never argue or get angry with anyone, even if someone is trying to pick a fight with you because he supports your opposition. If someone disagrees vehemently with your position, do not try to convince him otherwise. Tell him that everyone has the right to his own opinion, wish him a good day, and let him pass on by. The shopping-center staffers' job is to remind supporters to vote and to convince the undecided voter to vote for your side. A fist fight gets you newspaper coverage, but that is not the kind of headline that your campaign needs.

For outgoing, pleasant people, staffing shopping centers can be the most enjoyable part of the campaign. Friends and neighbors come by the table to say hello. Strangers wave and smile, encouraging your efforts. Sincerely curious voters ask questions that have long been puzzling them; they are grateful for the clarification. It is a lovely, animated, social time.

The public response to your presence will show you how effectively your campaign has been run until then. If your grassroots campaign has filled the newspapers with letters to the editor and sent out good mailers, then many people will already be on your side and appreciate the volunteers being there. They will provide plenty of encouragement.

Sometimes grassroots candidates themselves enjoy being

at a table near the entrance of a popular store in order to introduce themselves to voters and to pass out their own campaign brochures. This is a good method of meeting many people in a short period of time and is especially useful for a little-known candidate running against a well-known incumbent. A candidate may want to begin appearing at shopping centers early in the campaign and therefore get a jump on the other, more complacent people running for office. A candidate simply cannot afford to be shy about promoting himself.

What if your opposition wants to set up a table right next to yours? Never agree to this. Your opposing messages to the public will cancel out both of your efforts. Most large stores have two entrances. Come to some kind of peaceful agreement with your oposition: You agree to stand at one entrance while your opposition can locate at the other entrance. Generally, whoever arrives first has the right to choose the better entrance.

Just as important as the shopping-center staffers themselves are the people who coordinate the staffers. Your campaign may need only one person to organize staffers for all the shopping centers in town or you may choose to have one coordinator per shopping center.

The coordinator's job is to telephone all the volunteers who might be interested in staffing shopping centers. He will check your endorsement cards to find out who volunteered and which hours and days are best for each volunteer. He should explain to each volunteer exactly what shopping-center staffing involves and ask if the volunteer would prefer to staff a table alone or with a partner. If the person prefers a partner, the coordinator should ask if he knows anyone who would work with him. If not, then the coordinator should find a partner for him.

The coordinator must make certain that each shopping-center staffer knows what to take with him: a small card table, chair, signs, brochures, endorsement cards, bumperstickers, buttons, masking tape, paperweights, etc. The volunteer can pick up all of these items at campaign headquarters, which should have prepared boxes of these items for the staffers. If a staffer is unable to make it to campaign headquarters, then the coordinator should transport the table, chair, and campaign materials.

The coordinator also prepares a written schedule for every shopping center listing the times and people who will be volunteering during those hours. Don't wear out your volunteers. A three-hour session at a shopping center is plenty for one day. A sample schedule might be as follows. On a Saturday in front of a popular grocery store, Vanessa is scheduled from 10:00 A.M. to 1:00 P.M., followed by Tom from 1:00 P.M. to 4:00 P.M. When Tom arrives, the table, chair, signs, and brochures have already long been set up by Vanessa, who picked them up at campaign headquarters that morning before her shift began. So Tom merely takes over Vanessa's seat. However, at the end of his shift, it will be Tom's job to pack away the table, chairs, and paperwork and transport them all back to campaign headquarters (usually the candidate's living room).

The coordinator should visit every staffer's very first hour on the job to answer any questions, provide material if necessary, and give moral support. First-time volunteers are not quite sure what to say or do, but generally within the first fifteen minutes of encounters with passersby, they catch on quickly and warm to the job.

Finally, although volunteers are likely to be responsible, dedicated people, it is important for the coordinator to give them a reminder call the day before they are scheduled to staff a shopping center. Even well-meaning people can simply forget to show up. Volunteers usually welcome the extra reminder.

Precinct Walkers

Precinct walking involves pairs of campaign volunteers strolling around neighborhoods, knocking on doors, passing out brochures, and convincing people to vote for your candidate or cause. Precinct walking is tiring. That is one reason why it is best to walk neighborhoods in pairs—to keep up morale as you trudge up and down streets repeating the same campaign concerns to neighbor after neighbor. An efficient way of working in pairs is for one person to knock on doors on one side of the street, while the other person handles the opposite side of the street.

It is important to wear comfortable shoes that will carry your feet painlessly for miles. Just as important is your dress. You want people to open the door for you, so dress nicely. Casual dress is fine; there's no need for suits and ties. But do wear campaign buttons with your candidate's name clearly visible. You do not want residents to confuse you with a burglar or salesman.

What should you say when someone opens the front door? Introduce yourself immediately, giving your name. You have many doors to cover, so keep your speech simple and short. Also, you are probably interrupting the resident, who may be busy doing something and in no mood to hear a long-winded speech from a stranger.

A simple and effective introduction might be: "Hello, my name is Vince Volunteer. I'm campaigning for Chris Candidate for mayor. Have you considered voting for Chris?"

If the person answers, "Yes, I'm voting for Chris. She's a great leader," then just congratulate the person on his wise decision, give him the campaign literature, and bid a gracious farewell.

If the person answers, "I'm not sure who to vote for," then briefly give Chris's stance on the most important issues in your community and place the campaign packet in the voter's hand. Ask him to read it carefully because you are certain that he will agree that Chris is the best candidate for mayor.

If the person answers, "I can't abide Chris nor what she stands for!" and proceeds to elaborate on how awful she is, just thank him for his time, wish him a good day, and move on.

In some elections, the majority of people whom you will encounter may be undecided voters with lots of questions. Be patient with these folks and answer their questions as best you can. Refer them to the campaign brochures for further answers. A good technique is to ask them what local issues they care about most, then assure them that your candidate cares deeply about the same issues. (Of course, only say this if it is true!)

As you go door to door, very few people will invite you inside their homes. But to be on the safe side, even when that rare person does invite you inside, it is best to stay on the front porch. You never know when you happen to knock on the door of an unstable individual. So it's best to just thank the person politely for the invitation inside, but explain that you don't want to take up much of his time.

The whole point of precinct walking is to make personal contact with people, so if no one is home, then at least leave a campaign brochure by the front door. Tuck the brochure under a corner of the doormat or a flower pot or in the newspaper slot. Make sure that the brochure is protected from wind and rain. It will be tempting to put your campaign material inside people's mailboxes. But remember, mailbox stuffing is a federal offense, and an irate postal carrier may remove all of your brochures, stuff them in the trash, and even report you to the authorities. On the bright side, most postal carriers simply do not mind at all.

Weekends are the best time to catch people at home. After work hours, just before dinner, is also a good time.

Is precinct walking always possible? No, it is not. Precinct walking is difficult in rural areas where gates and dogs discourage intruders. The long distance between houses in rural areas also makes precinct walking too time-consuming and impractical. In addition, in large cities where apartments and condominiums predominate, it is often impossible to reach residents, who are reluctant to open their doors to strangers. Frankly, precinct walking works best in suburban neighborhoods where houses are accessible and close together.

Precinct walking is also very effective in business districts. Obviously, you want to visit the businesses during business hours. Moreover, the main concern of businesspeople is likely to be how your candidate's policies will impact the local economy. Even as an environmentalist, be prepared to supply some economic answers.

The coordinator in charge of organizing the precinct walking will prepare lists of streets for each pair of precinct walkers to cover. Be certain to check off the addresses right after you visit them. Beware: After an hour or two of precinct walking, all streets tend to look alike, and it is easy to forget what areas you already covered. So your address checklist can be invaluable in reminding you that you already visited a particular street two hours earlier.

In some very well organized campaigns, the precinct walker puts a mark by every address on the sheet indicating whether the resident was home and whether the resident was a supporter or undecided. This information can prove useful in forecasting victory or defeat. It also lets your campaign know what neighborhoods are more sympathetic to your side. That information can also be helpful when the telephone committee gets busy calling supporters to remind them to vote.

What campaign material should you hand out? This varies widely. But, in general, precinct walkers' packets may include:

- A brochure about your candidate.

- Copies of any outstanding newspaper editorials in favor of your candidate.

- A letter praising your candidate either from a notable public figure or respected organization.

- An endorsement card for the resident to fill out and mail in (hopefully, with a campaign contribution enclosed or an offer to volunteer in the campaign).

- A few bumperstickers and buttons to hand out in case anybody asks for them, as well as some signs (keep in your car nearby) for people who request them.

Should the candidate walk precincts? This is entirely up to the candidate. It is part of the American tradition for candidates to go door to door. But as we discussed above, in large cities and in rural communities precinct walking has its limitations. In those places, it is best for the candidate to focus on visiting the business districts, as well as appearing in busy shopping centers on weekends and after work to introduce himself directly to the voters. In many communities, this may be much more practical than precinct walking. In shopping centers, instead of the candidate walking to the voters, the voters come to him. It is less tiring than precinct walking and much more efficient. The candidate should have a complete campaign packet to hand to each voter with whom he chats.

Just as the shopping-center coordinator, the coordinator for precinct walking has primarily a telephone job. She must telephone volunteers, find out their schedules, and assign them neighborhoods to walk. Actually, precinct walkers have a great deal of flexibility to adapt precinct walking to their own schedules. For example, one energetic precinct walker used to stuff campaign brochures into her baby's perambulator and go door to door as part of her daily stroll with her newborn.

Telephone Bank

The campaign's telephone bank is the direct lifeline to volunteers and voters. The telephone bank should be organized at the outset of the campaign. Over time, it will grow and evolve.

The campaign may wish to assign someone to be the telephone bank coordinator. This must be a very well organized, reliable person because the job is an important one—so important that often the campaign director herself takes on this responsibility.

The first time that a telephone bank will be needed is in the preparation for the kick-off party. Callers must telephone for sponsors to bring food, drinks, and auction items. Calls are then made just before the kick-off to remind supporters to attend and to obtain a head count so that enough food and drinks will be on hand. At this early stage in the campaign, the telephone bank may consist mainly of the candidate, the campaign director, and a few close friends.

Once the endorsement cards start flowing in, your campaign will have a large pool of volunteers to tap for the telephone bank. After the kick-off party and the first mailer, your campaign will have a pile of endorsement cards filled out by supporters. The immediate task of the telephone bank is to call every supporter to find out for what task they are willing to volunteer: staffing a shopping center, precinct walking, working at campaign headquarters, writing letters to the editor, putting up signs, etc. While you are calling, make sure to get plenty of volunteers for the telephone bank.

The telephone bank's most important job—to get out the vote—takes place during the final weeks before the election. This telephoning to remind people to vote escalates to a feverish pitch the very last two weeks before election day.

It does your campaign no good to have a majority of your city supporting your candidate if they do not go to the polls to vote. Even popular candidates can lose elections because their supporters are so confident of their candidates' victory that the supporters do not bother to vote. Then these same supporters are shocked when their candidates lose!

This last-minute get-out-the-vote effort is very easy for callers because they will be telephoning only supporters. By the final weeks of the campaign, lists of supporters have been tabulated from the endorsement cards, precinct walkers' information sheets, frequent voters list, environmental organizations' lists, housing associations' lists, and other neighborhood associations' lists. Throughout the campaign, these lists of supporters grow steadily.

In your campaign, you are likely to have volunteers who have access to offices with several telephones. Lawyers, realtors, travel agents, and others often have roomy offices with plenty of telephone lines. Many of these offices are closed in the evenings and on weekends. During these off-hours, groups of volunteers can gather to telephone supporters. Provide good food and beverages for them. This is the finale of the campaign, and many volunteers will be tense and exhausted; so make the telephoning an enjoyable group activity.

For many people, it is more convenient to telephone from the comfort of their own homes. Provide these volunteers with lists of names and telephone numbers to call and let them call supporters as their own schedules permit.

Supply every telephone bank volunteer with a scripted statement of a paragraph or two, summarizing the importance of voting for your candidate. The script should flow naturally and be easy to read. Every volunteer can adapt the script to his or her own style.

Researchers

Your campaign researchers' job is to dig up useful information on the campaign issues and on your opponent. The information printed in your brochures and mailers should always be 100 percent accurate. It is up to your researchers to ascertain this accuracy. Their sources of information can include public records at city hall, newspaper files, and campaign financial statements. For example, your opponent may have a history of litigation because of shady business dealings and he may be affiliated with special-interest groups. All this takes digging to uncover.

Researchers also must investigate rumors about your opposition. Your campaign may hear a juicy rumor about your opponent, one that your candidate is dying to spring on him in his next public debate. But always exercise enough self-control to find documentation to prove the veracity of a rumor before you use it publicly. Never make wild, unsubstantiated accusations.

There may be some information uncovered by your researchers that is inappropriate for your campaign brochures. If you have such surplus information on your opponents, funnel it to your letter writers and have them discuss it through letters to the editor. Such information may involve some personal, professional, and political aspects of your opposition that have no place in brochures.

How many researchers do you need? If your researchers are competent, you may need only one or two. Good researchers enjoy rummaging through old newspapers and public records to find the exciting tidbits of information that may well bring victory to your campaign.

Keep spirits high! Ideally, your campaign will encourage mutual respect and harmony among all of your valuable volunteers so that a wonderful spirit of cooperation prevails. Such cooperation makes teamwork a pure joy. To keep morale high, the candidate should extend thanks to everyone—in private and in public. All human beings thrive on appreciation. Volunteers especially deserve plenty of praise. Thanks to them, environmental dreams become reality.

CHAPTER 13

Victory and Defeat

V ictories and losses await every environmental activist. It is important to savor each success and to learn useful lessons from every obstacle. Occasional disappointments are inevitable. However, today's setback may become the stepping-stone to tomorrow's victory.

Victory

Congratulations! You won! Your organization was victorious in preserving a lake, beach, grazing land, or precious desert. Your group successfully worked to create public open space or a new park. Your organization planted trees and wildflowers throughout your city. You defeated plans for a gigantic development proposal or a nuclear power plant. You saved a forest from herbicides and chainsaws. You stopped a factory from dumping toxics into your groundwater supply. Your election campaign put an environmentalist into public office. Whatever your environmental goal, no matter how large or small, you won! Bravo! It's time to celebrate.

Now that your organization has achieved its goals, throw a big bash for your members. Eat, drink, and be merry together. Your group has been working hard for months, perhaps years,

to succeed, and you all may be exhausted. But don't let your victory slip by without a celebration. You've earned it! It's time to pat yourselves proudly on the back for making grassroots democracy work in your community.

Plan a block party, a barbecue, a giant picnic, a potluck, a dance! Proclaim your victory in letters to the editor and in your organization's newsletter. Thank everyone for their participation, which made your success possible. Give special recognition to individuals who worked the hardest.

Frolic while you can, for your next environmental battle may be lurking just around the corner.

Naturally, all candidates hope to win the election. Thus, it is customary for candidates to plan a victory party for their supporters on election eve. The rejoicing is tearful with ecstasy when the local election office announces a clear victory for your candidate. It is time for celebrating and for the candidate to make a speech to thank all his loyal, hard-working supporters.

Where do you hold a candidate's victory party? Every penny of campaign funds should have been spent on the campaign itself, so there is likely to be no money left to rent a place for the party. Often, victory parties are held in the candidate's home, with supporters cheerfully squeezed into every square inch of living space.

If you expect a crowd too large for your candidate's home, then search for an alternate free site. You may belong to a club or community center that will offer their facilities for free. Perhaps one of your supporters owns a cafe or restaurant that he will offer gratis for your victory festivities.

How do you notify your candidate's supporters about the party? One of the last mailers of the campaign is an invitation to the victory party to be sent to your campaign workers and contributors in the final week before the election. Following is a sample victory party invitation:

YOU ARE INVITED TO
AN ELECTION NIGHT VICTORY PARTY
FOR
VICTORIA GREENWAY

Time: 8:00 P.M. to midnight on Tuesday, November 5

Place: Home of Victor and Victoria Greenway
        4 World Peace Avenue
        Jolly Green Junction, USA

Our campaign has spent every last penny on the election. So, dear friends, we request that you contribute the food and drinks. Please bring a platter of goodies or a bottle of your favorite beverage!

For the candidate, victory means that the real work is only just beginning. For campaign workers, too, the job continues.

It is important for candidates' followers to stay involved in community concerns—to support the new political leaders when they are right and to correct them when they err.

"The price of democracy is eternal vigilance," Thomas Jefferson stated. For grassroots activists, "eternal vigilance" is the price we gladly pay for the privilege of participating in democracy, determining our community's future, and preserving our environment.

Defeat

Sorry! Your candidate lost the election. One sure thing is that your postelection party will not be a barrel of laughs. At an election eve party where the candidate is not victorious, there is inevitably much wailing and gnashing of teeth. The party of a defeated candidate can resemble a wake as tears mingle with curses.

How does the defeated candidate feel? Rotten! He feels hurt and disappointed. The pain of defeat runs deep. The candidate will feel resentment toward the community's voters for not appreciating his worth and toward the victorious candidate for running a vicious campaign. He may also feel like hiding in a dark closet for a month until the emotional wounds heal. He is exhausted from the difficult campaign and embarrassed about losing.

How to rebound? First, the candidate must rest. He probably could use a change of scenery. Everything in town will remind him of his defeat. A short vacation—even a weekend away at a favorite fishing hole or a day of hiking in the woods—begins to restore his spirits.

Second, it is vital to remember that the candidate lost only one election. There are many elections to come.

Think of the future. Even defeat in an election may lead to new opportunities. Following are a few examples of how an unsuccessful candidate can snatch victory from the jaws of defeat.

• *Form an organization.*   During the campaign, the candidate has organized a group of loyal, hard-working, dedicated activists. After the election, the candidate can create an organization with this group and fight for the same issues the candidate would have endorsed if elected. Such an environmental organization may grow to have more far-reaching political power than any elected official could ever obtain.

• *Run for another office.* After an election, the candidate, even defeated, has gained tremendous name recognition and notoriety and can use this momentum to run for another political office. For example, a candidate who has run for governor unsuccessfully may still have gained a huge statewide following and might run victoriously for an opening in the U.S. Senate the following year. If a candidate loses a race for county supervisor, he can use the campaign's momentum to run for city council in the next election.

• *Use one's campaign reputation to obtain an influential position.* During the campaign, the candidate has championed environmental causes and proved himself a leader in the movement. Doors may now fly open for him to be appointed or elected to important positions within existing conservation organizations.

• *Run again for the same office.* If the candidate continues his grassroots activism in the intervening years between elections, then he may run again for the same office and win. Between elections, he enhances his reputation and experience by remaining an activist. In the next election he may well win a resounding victory!

Every activist will encounter defeats along with victories. The point is to keep your fighting spirit alive for the noble cause. Your victories will amply compensate for the occasional defeat. The marshland you saved from development will thank you with every bird that nests there. The hillside that you preserved as a park will thank you with every blade of grass that grows. The air and water that are cleaner because of your activism will be enjoyed by everyone.

Grassroots activism is its own reward. Life itself thanks you.

APPENDIX

National Environmental Organizations

N ational environmental organizations can supply you with much useful information. Some national groups even have activist regional chapters that can lend you direct support. Following is a partial list of national environmental organizations. Contact those groups that could help your particular cause.

Acid Rain Foundation, Inc.
1410 Varsity Drive
Raleigh, NC 27606
(919) 828-9443
   The foundation focuses on acid rain, global atmosphere, recycling, and forest ecosystems, and supplies educational resources.

Alliance for Environmental Education
10751 Ambassador Drive, Suite 201
Manassas, VA 22110
(703) 335-1025
   In partnership with the Environmental Protection Agency, the alliance is establishing a network of interactive environmental education centers based at colleges, universities, and institutions.

American Association of Zoological Parks and Aquariums
7970-D Old Georgetown Road
Bethesda, MD 20814
(301) 907-7777

This professional organization represents 156 accredited zoos and aquariums in North America. Its goal is to further wildlife conservation and education and to enforce a code of ethics for all zoological institutions. It emphasizes wildlife conservation through captive propagation.

American Forestry Association
P.O. Box 2000
Washington, DC 20013
(202) 667-3300

The association's purpose is to maintain trees and forests and to attract the interest of citizens, industry, and government to tree and forest resources through action-oriented programs. The emphasis is on Global Releaf, an international campaign to assist individuals, businesses, and governments to plant and care for trees.

American Geographical Society
156 Fifth Avenue, Suite 600
New York, NY 10010-7002
(212) 242-0214

The society publishes The Geographical Review *and* Focus *magazine. It provides educational travel programs, lecturers for educational and business audiences, and an award program to encourage research in geographical knowledge with an ecological emphasis.*

American Hiking Society
1015 31st Street NW
Washington, DC 20007
(703) 385-3252

The society is dedicated to protecting the interests of hikers and preserving America's footpaths. It maintains a public information service to provide hikers with facts regarding facilities, organizations, and best use of trails to protect the environment.

American Horse Protection Association, Inc.
1000 29th Street NW, Suite T-100
Washington, DC 20007
(202) 965-0500

The association is dedicated to the welfare of wild and domestic horses. It fights for the humane treatment of horses through litigation, investigation, and public awareness of proper horse care.

American Humane Association
P.O. Box 1266
Denver, CO 80201
(303) 792-9900
The association works to prevent abuse, cruelty, and neglect of children and animals.

American Pedestrian Association
P.O. Box 624
Forest Hills, NY 11375
This group works for the preservation and protection of pedestrian environments against vehicular encroachment of all types and relates environmental costs to vehicular traffic.

American Rivers
801 Pennsylvania Avenue SE, Suite 400
Washington, DC 20003
(202) 547-6900
This conservation organization is leading the effort to protect and restore the nation's outstanding rivers and their environments. It has preserved more than 10,000 river miles for clean water, threatened fish and wildlife, recreation, and scenic beauty. Its concerns include dams, diversions, channelization, and adverse development.

Animal Protection Institute of America
2831 Fruitridge Road
Sacramento, CA 95831
(916) 731-5521
The institute is dedicated to elimination of the pain and suffering inflicted on animals and to the preservation of threatened species.

Center for Environmental Information
46 Prince Street
Rochester, NY 14607
(716) 271-3550
The center offers a multifaceted program of publications, education programs, and information services and provides accurate, comprehensive information on environmental issues.

Center for Marine Conservation
1725 DeSales Street NW, Suite 500
Washington, DC 20036
(202) 429-5609
This group is devoted to the conservation of marine wildlife, their habitats, and fisheries. It works to prevent marine pollution and to protect endangered species and promotes marine biodiversity.

Center for Plant Conservation
P.O. Box 299
St. Louis, MO 63166
(314) 577-9450
The center conserves rare and endangered native plants through research, cultivation, and education at botanical gardens and arboreta in the United States. It establishes off-site germplasm collections in the National Collection of Endangered Plants.

Center for Science Information
4252 20th Street
San Francisco, CA 94114
(415) 553-8772
The center informs journalists and decision makers about the environmental applications of biotechnology.

Citizens' Clearinghouse for Hazardous Wastes, Inc.
P.O. Box 926
Arlington, VA 22216
(703) 276-7070
The clearinghouse is directed by Lois Marie Gibbs, founder of the Love Canal Homeowners Association in Niagara Falls, New York. Gibbs organized a small, blue-collar community and successfully took on city hall, the state, and the White House to bring the improper disposal of hazardous wastes to national prominence. The Citizens' Clearinghouse is a national organization providing practical grassroots advice for communities dealing with hazardous waste problems.

Clean Water Action
1320 18th Street NW
Washington, DC 20036
(202) 457-1286
This national citizens' organization is working for control of toxic

chemicals, protection of wetlands, groundwater, and coastal waters, and safe solid-waste management.

The Cousteau Society, Inc.
930 W. 21st Street
Norfolk, VA 23517
(804) 627-1144
The society was founded in 1973 by Jacques Cousteau in the belief that an informed public makes the best choices for a healthy planet. It produces television films, books, and membership publications and offers lectures and a summer field-study program.

Defenders of Wildlife
1244 19th Street NW
Washington, DC 20036
(202) 659-9510
This organization focuses on protecting and restoring habitats and wildlife communities, reducing environmental hazards to wildlife, and promoting wildlife appreciation and education. Its specific projects include restoring the grey wolf to its former range in Yellowstone National Park, preventing entanglement of marine mammals in plastic debris and discarded fish nets, and working with Congress to develop a bill to strengthen the National Wildlife Refuge System.

Ducks Unlimited, Inc.
One Waterfowl Way
Long Grove, IL 60647
(708) 438-4300
The group's goal is to enhance wetland ecosystems in North America.

Earth Island Institute
300 Broadway, Suite 28
San Francisco, CA 94133
(415) 788-3666
The institute's current programs include the International Marine Mammal Project, Sea Turtle Restoration Project, Baikal Watch, Urban Habitat Program, and International Green Circle. The group stresses innovative projects for the preservation and restoration of the global environment.

Earthwatch
P.O. Box 403N
680 Mt. Auburn Street
Watertown, MA 02272
(617) 926-8200

Earthwatch sends volunteers to assist scientists around the world who are working to save rainforests and endangered species, to preserve archeological finds, and to study pollution effects.

Environmental Data Research Institute
797 Elmwood Avenue
Rochester, NY 14620
(716) 473-3090

The institute provides the environmental community with information on organizations, publications, and funding. It maintains a comprehensive data base on grants: who's giving money, who's getting it, where it goes, and for what purpose.

Environmental Defense Fund
257 Park Avenue South
New York, NY 10010
(212) 505-2100

This organization combines science, economics, and law to create viable solutions to ecological problems and publishes an excellent newsletter.

Fish and Wildlife Reference Service
5430 Grosvenor Lane, Suite 110
Bethesda, MD 20814
(301) 492-6403

The service is a computerized information clearinghouse supplying fish and wildlife management research reports.

Friends of the Earth
218 D Street SE
Washington, DC 20003
(202) 544-2600

These environmental advocates lobby in Washington, D.C., and in state capitals for environmental issues and publish an award-winning magazine. Among the group's concerns are ozone depletion, agricultural biotechnology, toxic chemical safety, groundwater protection, and coal strip-mining abuses.

The Fund for Animals
200 W. 57th Street
New York, NY 10019
(212) 246-2096

This group opposes cruelty to wild and domestic animals and works to oppose all sport hunting, to limit the breeding of domestic animals, and to preserve rare species.

Greenpeace USA
1436 U Street NW
Washington, DC 20009
(202) 462-1177

This well-known direct-action organization has offices in twenty-four countries. Its prime concerns include global warming, ozone depletion, international waste trade, nuclear weapons production, marine mammals, and endangered animals. It also works to reduce toxic and nuclear waste.

Hawkwatch International, Inc.
P.O. Box 35706
1420 Carlisle NE, Suite 100
Albuquerque, NM 87176-5706
(505) 255-7622

The organization is dedicated to the conservation of birds of prey and their habitats in the western United States through research and public education. It supports six field projects to monitor trends and migration patterns of migratory raptors in the Rocky Mountains.

The Humane Society of the United States
2100 L Street NW
Washington, DC 20037
(202) 452-1100

The society works to prevent cruelty to all living creatures. Special attention is given to the proper care of domesticated animals.

Inform
381 Park Avenue South
New York, NY 10016
(212) 689-4040

This is an environmental research and education organization that reports on practical actions for conservation. Its research includes hazardous waste reduction, garbage management, urban air quality, and land and water conservation.

Institute for Conservation Leadership
2000 P Street NW, Suite 413
Washington, DC 20036
(202) 466-3330
The institute's goal is to increase the number and effectiveness of volunteer organizations and community leaders. It provides leadership training and organizational development programs.

Institute for Earth Education
P.O. Box 288
Warrenville, IL 60555
(509) 395-2299
Through its worldwide network of branches, the institute conducts workshops, provides a seasonal journal, hosts international and regional conferences, supports local groups, distributes an annual catalogue, and publishes books and program materials.

International Fund for Animal Welfare
411 Main Street
Yarmouth Port, MA 02675
(508) 362-4944
This international animal welfare organization is dedicated to protecting wild and domestic animals from cruelty. It is interested in the preservation of harp and hood seals in Canada, dog and cat abuse in the Philippines, elephants in Africa, the use of animals in lab testing, and the welfare of whales and other marine mammals.

Island Press
1718 Connecticut Avenue NW, Suite 300
Washington, DC 20009
1-800-828-1302
Island Press publishes environmental sourcebooks on agriculture, global warming, forestry, hazardous waste, land use, water and wetlands, and wildlife. Ask for a free catalogue of books.

The Land and Water Fund of the Rockies
1405 Arapahoe, Suite 200
Boulder, CO 80302
(303) 444-1188
This organization provides free legal aid to grassroots environmental groups in Arizona, Colorado, Idaho, Montana, New Mexico, Utah, and Wyoming. Local volunteer attorneys offer advice and counsel and will litigate for client groups.

The Land Trust Alliance
900 17th Street NW, Suite 410
Washington, DC 20006
(202) 785-1410

The alliance is a national organization of local and regional land conservation groups that provides programs and services to help land trusts reach their full potential. It provides educational materials and technical assistance for land trusts and other land conservation professionals.

National Arbor Day Foundation
211 N. 12th Street, Suite 501
Lincoln, NE 68508
(402) 474-5655

This educational organization is dedicated to tree planting and conservation and promotes programs such as Trees of America, Tree City USA, Conservation Trees, and Celebrate Arbor Day.

National Audubon Society
950 Third Avenue
New York, NY 10022
(212) 832-3200

The society's staff of scientists, lobbyists, lawyers, policy analysts, and educators work through field and policy research, lobbying, litigation, and citizen action to protect habitats throughout the Americas. This effective, grassroots organization has many regional chapters.

National Coalition Against the Misuse of Pesticides
701 Edwards Street SW, Suite 200
Washington, DC 20003
(202) 543-5450

This is a national network committed to pesticide safety and the adoption of alternative pest-management strategies that reduce or eliminate dependency on toxic chemicals. Its emphasis is on local action and community-based organizations.

National Wildflower Research Center
2600 FM 973 N.
Austin, TX 78725
(512) 929-3600

The center studies North American wildflowers and other native plants with the aim of reestablishing native plants in landscapes.

National Wildlife Federation

1400 16th Street NW
Washington, DC 20036
(202) 797-6800

The NWF distributes periodicals and educational materials, sponsors outdoor education programs, and litigates environmental disputes. Its interests include forests, energy, toxic pollution, biotechnical fisheries, wetlands, water resources, and public lands.

Natural Resources Defense Council

40 W. 20th Street
New York, NY 10011
(212) 727-2700

The NRDC combines legal action, scientific research, and citizen education in a highly effective environmental protection program. Its major accomplishments have been in the areas of energy policy and nuclear safety, air and water pollution, urban transportation issues, pesticides and toxic substances, forest protection, and global warming.

The Nature Conservancy

1815 N. Lynn Street
Arlington, VA 22209
(703) 841-5300

This is an international organization committed to preserving biological diversity by protecting lands and the plants and animals that live there. The conservancy manages a system of more than 1100 nature sanctuaries. It works for land protection in fifty states in the United States and in twelve countries in Latin America.

North American Native Fishes Association

123 W. Mt. Airy Avenue
Philadelphia, PA 19119
(215) 247-0384

The association encourages increased scientific observation, study, and research to assemble and distribute information about native fishes.

Nuclear Information and Resource Service

1424 16th Street NW, Suite 601
Washington, DC 20036
(202) 328-0002

The service acts as a networking and information clearinghouse for environmental activists concerned with nuclear power and waste issues. It provides citizens with the information and tools necessary to challenge nuclear facilities and policies.

Pacific Whale Foundation
101 N. Kihei Road
Kihei, HI 96753
(808) 879-8860

The foundation conducts field research worldwide and assists government and nongovernment agencies in developing conservation policies and plans for endangered marine life. It also offers education and conservation programs.

Population Crisis Committee
1120 19th Street NW, Suite 550
Washington, DC 20036
(202) 659-1833

The committee's goal is to stimulate public awareness and action toward reducing population growth rates. It advocates universal and voluntary access to family planning services to achieve world population stabilization and emphasizes the relationship between population growth and environmental degradation.

Population-Environment Balance
1325 G Street NW, Suite 1003
Washington, DC 20005
(202) 879-3000

This national nonprofit organization is dedicated to education and advocacy of measures to encourage population stabilization in the United States in order to safeguard the environment.

Rails-to-Trails Conservancy
1400 16th Street NW, Suite 300
Washington, DC 20036
(202) 797-5400

The conservancy is converting thousands of miles of abandoned railroad corridors to public trails for walking, bicycling, horseback riding, cross-country skiing, wildlife habitat, and nature appreciation.

Rainforest Action Network
301 Broadway, Suite A
San Francisco, CA 94133
(415) 398-4404

This activist organization works internationally in cooperation with other environmental and human rights organizations on major campaigns to protect rainforests.

Rainforest Alliance
270 Lafayette, Suite 512
New York, NY 10012
(212) 941-1900

The alliance's primary mission is to develop and promote sound alternatives to deforestation and opportunities for people to utilize tropical forests without destroying them.

The René Dubos Center for Human Environments, Inc.
100 E. 85th Street
New York, NY 10028
(212) 249-7745

This is an independent education and research organization founded by the scientist René Dubos to focus on the social and humanistic aspects of environmental problems. The center's mission is to develop creative policies for the resolution of environmental conflicts and to help decision makers and the general public formulate new environmental values. It offers educational programs for teacher trainers and business/industry on environmental quality and responsibility.

Renew America
1400 16th Street NW, Suite 710
Washington, DC 20036
(202) 232-2252

This group provides information and recommendations to policy makers, media, and other environmental organizations. It promotes success stories to be used as models throughout the country and presents awards to honor those working to solve environmental problems.

Save-the-Redwoods League
114 Sansome Street, Room 605
San Francisco, CA 94104
(415) 362-2352

The organization purchases redwood groves and watershed lands for protection in public parks and supports reforestation, research, and educational programs.

Save the Whales, Inc.
P.O. Box 2397
1426 Main Street, Unit E
Venice, CA 90291
(310) 392-6226

This group educates children and adults about marine mammals, their environment, and their preservation. Save the Whales is beginning educational programs via a mobile unit (Whales on Wheels) that brings lectures to schoolchildren.

Scenic America
216 7th Street SE
Washington, DC 20003
(202) 546-1100

The organization works to protect America's scenic landscapes and to clean up visual pollution. It provides information and technical assistance on billboard and sign control, scenic areas preservation, growth management, and all forms of aesthetic regulation.

Sierra Club
730 Polk Street
San Francisco, CA 94109
(415) 776-2211

The Sierra Club promotes conservation of the natural environment by influencing public policy decisions—legislative, administrative, legal, and electoral. It has active state and local chapters for extensive volunteer participation.

Sierra Club Legal Defense Fund
180 Montgomery Street, Suite 1400
San Francisco, CA 94104-4230
(415) 627-6700

This group provides legal advice, counsel, and litigation for environmental causes nationwide.

Soil and Water Conservation Society
7515 N.E. Ankeny Road
Ankeny, IA 50021-9764
(515) 289-2331

The society advocates the conservation of soil, water, and related natural resources.

Student Conservation Association, Inc.
P.O. Box 550
Charlestown, NH 03603
(603) 826-4301

Student and adult volunteers in the association serve in national parks, national forests, wildlife refuges, and other public or private conservation areas nationwide. It publishes Earth Work, *a magazine for current and future conservation professionals.*

Union of Concerned Scientists
26 Church Street
Cambridge, MA 02238
(617) 547-5552

This is an independent nonprofit organization of scientists and others concerned about the impact of advanced technology on society. It is concerned primarily with energy and arms. The energy program focuses on global warming, national energy policy, renewable energy, transportation, and nuclear power safety.

University Research Expeditions Program
University of California
Berkeley, CA 94720
(510) 642-6586

In cooperation with scientists from developing nations, the program supports projects focused on preserving the earth's resources and improving people's lives.

The Wilderness Society
900 17th Street
Washington, DC 20006
(202) 833-2300

The society works to protect wildlands and wildlife and to safeguard the integrity of our federal public lands, national forests, wildlife refuges, national seashores, recreation areas, and public domain lands.

Wildlife Conservation International
Division of the New York Zoological Society
Bronx, NY 10460
(212) 220-6891

The organization's goal is to help preserve the earth's biological diversity and ecosystems. It addresses conflicts between humans and wildlife and explores locally sustainable solutions, as well as providing grants for graduate students and professionals in wildlife sciences. The group has 122 projects in forty-six countries.

The Wildlife Society
5410 Grosvenor Lane
Bethesda, MD 20814
(301) 897-9770

The society provides current scientific and management information on wildlife resources. Its programs include publishing scientific journals and books, providing certification and professional development programs, sponsoring meetings and workshops, enhancing wildlife curricula at colleges and universities, and providing policy makers with scientific information on wildlife conservation issues.

World Resources Institute
1709 New York Avenue NW, Suite 700
Washington, DC 20006
(202) 638-6300

This research and policy institute helps governments, the private sector, environmental and development organizations, and others address a fundamental question: How can societies meet human needs and nurture economic growth while preserving the natural resources and environmental integrity on which life and economic vitality depend? Its concerns include forests, biodiversity, economics, technology, climate, energy, and pollution.

Zero Population Growth
1400 16th Street NW, Suite 320
Washington, DC 20036
(202) 332-2200

This organization strives to achieve a sustainable balance among the earth's population, environment, and resources. Its primary activities include publishing newsletters and research reports, developing in-school population and education programs, and coordinating local and national citizen-action efforts.

BIBLIOGRAPHY

A Blueprint for Lobbying: A Citizen's Guide to the Politics of Preservation. Preservation Action, 1700 Connecticut Avenue, N.W., Suite 401, Washington, D.C. 20009. 1984. 40 pages.

Brigham, Nancy, with Dick Cluster and Ann Raszmann. **How to Do Leaflets, Newsletters and Newspapers.** Hastings House Publishers, New York, 1982. Order from PEP Publishers, P.O. Box 289, Essex Station, Boston, MA 02112. 110 pages.

Cone, Arthur Lambert, Jr. **How to Create and Use Solid Gold Fundraising Letters.** Fund-Raising Institute, Box 365, Ambler, PA 19002. 1987.

Cooke, Holland. **How to Keep Your Press Release Out of the Wastebasket.** Holland Cooke Seminars, Washington, D.C., 1988. Order from Holland Cooke, 3220 N Street, N.W., Washington, D.C. 20007. 130 pages.

Cooper-Hewitt Museum. **Urban Open Spaces.** Rizzoli, New York, 1981. 128 pages.

Flanagan, Joan. **Successful Fundraising: A Complete Handbook for Volunteers and Professionals.** Contemporary Books, 180 North Michigan Avenue, Chicago, IL 60601. 1991. 302 pages.

Freudenberg, Nicholas. **Not in Our Backyards! Community Action for Health and the Environment.** Monthly Review Press, 155 West 23rd Street, New York, NY 10011. 1984. 304 pages.

Gibbs, Lois Marie, with Will Collette. **Leadership Handbook on Hazardous Waste.** Citizens' Clearinghouse for Hazardous Wastes, P.O. Box 926, Arlington, VA 22216. 1983. 59 pages.

Gratz, Barbara Brandes. **The Living City.** Simon & Schuster, New York, 1989. 414 pages.

Hart, John. **Farming on the Edge: Saving Family Farms in Marin County, California.** University of California Press, Berkeley, California, 1991. 174 pages.

Klein, Kim. **Fundraising for Social Change.** Chardon Press, P.O. Box 101, Inverness, CA 94937. 1988. 202 pages.

Unterman, Richard K. **Accommodating the Pedestrian: Adapting Towns and Neighborhoods for Walking and Bicycling.** Van Nostrand Reinhold, New York, 1984. 232 pages.